Garden Transformations

Garden Transformations
DESIGNER SECRETS AND TRICKS OF THE TRADE

Bunny Guinness

David & Charles

To my father,
for his *joie de vivre*

A DAVID & CHARLES BOOK

Hardback edition first published in the UK in 1999
Paperback edition first published in the UK in 2002

Distributed in North America by F&W Publications, Inc.
4700 E. Galbraith Rd, Cincinnati, OH 45236
1-800-289-0963

ISBN 0 7153 1357 6

Please note: Great care has been taken to ensure that the information
contained in this book is both accurate and complete. However, since the
skills and competence of individuals vary widely, and no book of this
nature can replace specialist advice in appropriate cases, neither the
author nor the publisher can accept legal responsibility or liability for any
loss or damage caused by reliance upon the accuracy of such information.
Illustrations pages 12, 16, 18, 20, 22, 23, 48, 49 (top), 62, 65, 106,
112, 122, 130, 131 copyright © Martin Rodgers, all other illustrations
copyright © Bunny Guinness

Book designed by Peter Bennett

Printed in China by Dai Nippon
for David & Charles
Brunel House   Newton Abbot   Devon

ACKNOWLEDGMENTS

Firstly, I would like to thank all those gardeners who have created the many
different outdoor spaces illustrated and allowed me to photograph and include
these pictures in this book. Particular thanks are due to my clients, who have
worked with me to produce something a little different, and given me permission
to feature the results.

Particularly I wish to thank Prince and Princess Galitzine, Portmeirion Village,
Stephen Cooke and Nia Morris, Wyevale Garden Centres plc, Sir Roy Strong,
Michael Balston, Alan Gray and Graham Robeson, Mr Barry Townsley and the
Right Honourable Laura Townsley, William and Merry Proby, Molly and Robert
Wheatley, Bas and Jane Clarke, Ben Wilson, Ian Hamilton Finlay, Andrew de
Candole, the late David Hicks, Roger Murray-Leach, Sue and John Wimpeney,
Richard Foxcroft, Jean-Louis Germain, Anna Simond, Nick Rust, Ivan Hicks,
Honor Gibbs, Mike Harvey, Hatton Fruit Garden and Edmund Brudenell.

Several people have been particularly helpful in the production of this book and
deserve much credit and thanks. Anna Mumford, the editor, whose enthusiasm
and commitment never appeared to flag from start to finish; Christine Rista, who
was responsible for picture research, some editing and was unbelievably helpful
and fun to work with; Peter Bennett, the art director for his creativity,
perseverance and hard work and Mike Trier, whose help with the editing of the
treehouse and gypsy caravan construction demonstrated, yet again, his patience,
skill and professionalism.

I must give enormous thanks to Martin Rodgers for his help throughout the
paint effect step-by-step projects and at the eleventh hour with many of the
illustrations. As usual, he produced exactly what was required even though he had,
at times, to match my immature style rather than use his own, far superior skills.
Also I would like to thank Karine Floc'h of Cornelissen and Son Ltd for her advice
on paint effects.

David Harrison was extremely helpful with the construction step-by-steps. His
ever-practical input combined with his technical knowledge was indispensable.
Colin Leftley deserves great credit for his clear photographic coverage of these
same step-by-step projects and I extend my thanks to him.

I am grateful to Marianne Majerus for her great pictures and for putting up with
me on our photographic excursions.

Bob Weighton, the architect, deserves special mention and thanks as my
occasional sounding board and advisor. His natural eye for detail and depth of
technical knowledge has proved the difference between order and chaos.

Finally, I am indebted to my long-suffering husband and my children, Unity and
Freddie, who have had to develop greatly their skills in self-sufficiency and
frequently tolerate a fraught and fractured family life. Without their contributions
and support this book would never have materialized.

Contents

Introduction

There are so many exciting influences affecting garden design today: artists and sculptors, craftsmen, ecologists, interior designers, fashion gurus, architects, landscape architects now join the band of horticulturalists and garden designers to bring changes to the look of gardens. These vastly different disciplines contribute a whole new range of skills to the business of garden design and also a whole new way of looking at gardens. In this book, I have taken a selection of work by professionals from a range of disciplines and have tried to explain how they have achieved their unique effects.

For the last six years, I have been lucky enough to be asked to design a garden for The Chelsea Flower Show. The first time one produces one of these show gardens involves a steep learning curve, and on the first occasion I learned much from watching the other twenty or so gardens come together, day by day, at the show ground. Specialist painters, decorators, designers, craftsmen of many, many different trades, artists and sculptors all work intensively together injecting their particular skills. Visitors to The Chelsea Flower Show who view the gardens from a distance beyond the ropes cannot hope to assimilate all the intricate details, nor in many cases is it possible to work out how certain effects have been achieved. After the Show, people ask me about the details of my garden: how were the walls made to look so well aged? Who manufacturers the pea green used on the fence posts? Where do you get hold of good sculpture? How was the willow arbour constructed? I have endeavoured to answer many of these questions here, relating to many of the more unusual effects which come not just from my gardens but also those of other designers.

This year I was delighted to be asked to design a garden for the 1999 Chelsea Flower Show for Portmeirion Village (with Wyevale Garden Centres plc). They want the garden to be a cameo of their spectacular Italianate village in North Wales, designed by the late Sir Clough Williams Ellis. It has been fascinating to discover how this talented architect achieved the multiplicity of special effects, and I have included some of his ideas here.

When I first started studying Landscape Architecture, one of the most important things I learnt was to 'dig with my eyes'. When looking at gardens your initial response may be positive or negative, it may sweep you off your feet or leave you cold. However, if you leave aside your subjective reaction and bring in your analytical side you can then try and work out why a garden, or aspect of it, works or fails and, if it does work, how it has been achieved.

Many gardeners encounter difficulties when they are struggling with their own plots: 'I know it's not right, but I don't know what to do to get it right' is probably the phrase I hear most often, second only to 'I do not have a clue what to do with this area'. In this book, I have tried not only to show innovative elements and solutions which contribute to the make-up of a successful space but also to explain how and why they work so that they can be applied in a different context. Inevitably, the vast majority of illustrations shown are designed by professional designers from one of the many related fields. These are people who are intrigued by design and spend much of their working time pursuing their goals with a passion. Their wonderful results can often be frustrating, so I have endeavoured to clarify the 'magic ingredients' so that gardeners can replicate the ideas at home.

The book is made up of the topics that I find particularly useful and tend to give great emphasis to in my day to day work. First and foremost in my view is 'Transforming Problem Sites' (page 152). I firmly believe that as the house is often the focal point of a garden you should make it look its best — and more often than not there are imperfections that need to be disguised as well as positive elements that could be further enhanced. A garden can without doubt transform a house, and this is usually my starting point. The use of colour on hard surfaces (page 8) opens huge possibilities in ensuring that whatever the season, no garden looks bleak and dejected. Salvage is tremendous fun — the thrill, and satisfaction after a long quest, of finding something for next to nothing to create a unique effect is second to none. Other important garden elements such as paint effects, water, the play element, boundaries, surfaces, buildings and last, but certainly not least, plants, feature in most gardens and I have tried to show how rewarding it is to push back the boundaries of what is normally considered possible. In this way it is possible to achieve highly individual, sometimes quirky, results that straightaway transform and add a particular focus to a garden.

colour

OF ALL THE MATERIALS
AVAILABLE TO THE LAND-
SCAPE GARDENER, COLOUR
APPLIED TO HARD SURFACES
IS ONE OF THE MOST EXCITING. COLOUR
WILL DICTATE THE MOOD OF A SPACE,
GIVING IT A STRONG IDENTITY; WHILE
BLUES HAVE A CALMING EFFECT, VIBRANT
YELLOWS INDUCE A LIVELY, EVEN
AGGRESSIVE FEEL. ON A PRACTICAL
LEVEL, COLOUR CAN BE USED TO MAKE
INTERESTING FEATURES PROMINENT OR
EYESORES RETREAT. BY COORDINATING
COLOUR WITHIN A GARDEN IT IS POS-
SIBLE TO UNIFY DISPARATE ELEMENTS
AND CREATE A COHESIVE SPACE. FINALLY,
COLOUR APPLIED TO HARD SURFACES
WILL SUPPORT THE EPHEMERAL COLOUR
SUPPLIED BY FOLIAGE AND FLOWERS
THROUGHOUT THE YEAR AND PROLONG
THE PRESENCE OF COLOUR, BRINGING
LIFE TO YOUR GARDEN DURING THE
LONG WINTER MONTHS.

COLOUR ON HARD SURFACES

Gardeners have always been fascinated with colour, and thousands of words have been written on plant colour combinations. Far less has been said about the opportunities afforded by colour applied to hard surfaces, yet they open up a whole new world of spectacular special effects that can magically transform a garden at very little cost and with minimal effort.

Colour has a strong emotional impact and produces an immediate sensory response. It is little surprise, then, that it has been used for centuries in the architectural and landscape context to add distinction, style and cohesion to designs. The Romans decorated ornaments, pavilions, fountains, subterranean porticoes and grottoes with brilliant glass mosaics. In India, the Far East and the Middle East, gilding was used to cover wooden ornaments and occasionally the roofs of important buildings. Brilliant blues, greens and gold were applied to eye-catching heraldic shields and crests throughout the medieval period. In Europe, from the fifteenth century onwards, fashionable house owners started painting their properties in the many bright, bold hues which started to become available. Brightly decorated garden buildings were erected solely to provide visual pleasure, as exemplified by the ornately and colourfully tiled pavilion in Old Moorish style that was built at Kew Gardens, Surrey, in the 1750s.

Previous generations seem to have been more adventurous with colour than we are today. Although they had a limited range of pigments to choose from, they made the most of them by mixing them and by juxtaposing interesting combinations. The advent of synthetic paint pigments in the twentieth century has hugely increased the options available. Interestingly, this seems to have made us more conservative in our choices, as if daunted by the enormous variety with which we are faced. We should derive comfort from the fact that paintwork is relatively inexpensive to change and start to experiment freely. There is really nothing to lose and, when it works, adventurous hard colour in the garden is truly spectacular.

Many gardeners study colour wheels when deciding what to choose, but it is all too easy to become hidebound by rules and the resulting compositions can be very flat. Many great paintings juxtapose colours which are technically inharmonious, and it is that very juxtaposition which brings them to life. So throw away the rule book and do not overlook the more natural colours because everything has colour of some sort, even neutrals, blacks, whites and greens.

In a garden, the impact of a certain colour can change dramatically, depending on light, surface, humidity and distance. So although the paint suppliers' charts that show a tiny, shiny spot of pigment surrounded by a white background are better than nothing they are fairly poor indicators of how the colour will look in a specific situation. Get hold of some sample testers and paint up some timber offcuts. Leave them lying around for a few days in different settings and take note of how they perform partly obscured by foliage, in bright sunlight, and on dull, wet days.

Colour in the garden has four main functions: it can attract attention to something; it can deceive by playing tricks with scale or camouflaging eyesores; it can stimulate

ABOVE *The clever and bold use of colour on this mosaic swan, created by the Romans in the fourth century AD, illustrates the importance of bold colours in the past.*

RIGHT *There is a tendency to think that historically the use of external colours was much tamer than it is today. This illustration of the Dome of the Rock in Jerusalem, which was built in AD685–91, shows that strong eye-catching colours were used on important buildings to embellish them and to increase their prominence.*

a certain emotion and create a particular mood; and, last but not least, it can decorate and embellish.

Colours may be warm or cold, light or heavy, soft or hard, and they may engender feelings of excitement or harmony. So the choice of a colour scheme is an important decision which will define the mood of the outdoor space that you are creating. Before making a decision on colour, try to analyse what you are trying to achieve in the garden and the obvious colour scheme will then present itself. Reds contribute vibrancy and warmth, greens tranquillity, and blues mystery and depth. To further complicate matters, hues tend to fade and weather, often becoming more harmonious with their surroundings as seasons progress but sometimes losing the positive 'bite' that encouraged you to choose them in the first place.

HISTORIC COLOURS

Historically, buildings were made from locally available materials, and this was true too of paints and limewash, which were coloured with local natural pigments. This ensured that the architecture blended harmoniously with the landscape in a coherent way. Nowhere is there a more perfect example of this than in Siena, Italy, where the warm yellows, ochres and reds of the houses are echoed in the soil and rocks of the surrounding hills — the overall effect is magical.

Unfortunately, following the introduction of synthetic pigments and the increased ease of transport, use of materials is no longer restricted to the region in which they originate. As a result, strident colour introductions often occur in towns and villages, breaking up the local identity and sense of cohesion. The worst examples are sometimes described as 'colour pollution' because of the alien element that they introduce.

It is useful to learn a lesson from history, and attempt to harmonize both house and garden with the immediate surroundings. Colour can be a useful tool for this: doors, windows and walls can all be easily returned to more authentic hues without the necessity of incurring great expense.

Paint Suppliers

Until the twentieth century, natural pigments which were taken from the earth, such as burnt umber, Italian ochre, Mars red and terra-verte, formed the basis of most paint colours. Today, several firms market paint ranges based on these pigments, producing colours of great subtlety. Despite their historic references, even these paints are manufactured using synthetic pigments, which have been chemically manufactured to match the colour of natural pigments. Synthetic pigments are cheaper than natural pigments (some of which are toxic), and by using them it is easier to control the consistency of shades produced, and to predict their resistance to weathering and fading. The subtle hues are achieved by mixing up to five colours together, rather than the usual two or three that more standard colours might employ. The greater complexity in their make-up imbues them with an intensity which is particularly effective when used outdoors.

Note that specialist paint suppliers usually charge a fee for their colour charts, which are often hand-painted. I feel the end results justify this modest initial outlay. The authenticity of some of these 'modern traditional hues' is sometimes in dispute. Inevitably shades have changed over time, and it is impossible to know exactly what the original looked like when first applied.

In terms of practical use in the modern garden, the colours are subtle, but they do not lack brilliance.

TOP *In the past the use of local building materials together with paints and washes derived from locally extracted pigments ensured that buildings blended in with the surrounding hues of the landscape. Today increased mobility of building products and huge ranges of colours have inevitably led to incohesive mixes of materials and colour pollution in many areas.*

Blue

Mauve   *Lilac blue*   *Grey blue*   *Oxford blue*   *Midnight blue*   *Cornflower blue*

Blue engenders feelings of mystery, complexity and depth. Large expanses of it are rarely found in nature unless you live near the sea and it is particularly elusive in northern Europe where blue skies are by no means commonplace, so extensive areas of saturated blue can look very obtrusive in many gardens. However, when used on a small scale, for example on fences, railings and pergolas, it can really work. Blue is an increasingly popular theme for cultivated herbaceous plants and bulbs, or in areas devoted to wild flowers. The soft, organic blues of the plants are lifted and emphasized by adding touches of 'hard' blue to plant supports, containers and other structural elements.

Blue is the ideal colour for anchoring a water feature to the garden and imbuing it with an air of permanence. Blue is thought of as a cold colour indoors and it is this coolness that makes it work well in the garden when trying to bond pools, cascades and streams to surrounding areas of vegetation. Try positioning a blue seat by a pool, surrounded by plantings of blue *Brunnera macrophylla;* you will be surprised at what a difference such a simple step makes. At the end of a hot, dusty summer, when foliage and flowers are fading, blue fixtures and fittings will add freshness and energy to the garden as well as enhancing the remnants of blue flower colour that remain.

Blue is often associated with hot tropical climates, Mediterranean terraces and Moorish courtyards, and gardeners in cooler countries find it difficult to use it, particularly in its saturated form. While it looks terrific on a hot summer's day against bright greens and brilliant sunshine, it becomes too dominant in winter when set against the drabness of the brown dormant plantings and the grey skies. You can counteract this effect in different ways. One way is to limit its use to moveable features such as pots, which you can take indoors in winter. Another method is to soften its impact by mixing the blue with whites and greys before applying it or by 'distressing' it, sponging it, or applying various other paint techniques (see pages 26–45). Alternatively, use it in parts of the garden that are seen only in summer, or in small areas which are heavily planted, so the spots of colour are well camouflaged.

Blue is a rewarding colour that complements most building materials: stone, brick, slate, gravel, timber, stainless steel, render and concrete. The colour swatch shows six shades which I use regularly. Of these, the most classic and understated are the dark midnight blues that look so elegant on Versailles tubs, timber pergolas and the front doors of Georgian houses in the British Isles. I especially like using Dulux's Midnight 7415-R82B. The calmness of grey-blue works well with mellow stonework and particularly with honey colours – I favour Berrington Blue No. 14 made by Farrow & Ball. Cornflower blues are at their best seen against warm skies, but will tolerate cooler surroundings provided they are used in limited areas. Lilac blue is a little cooler and more purplish; it is a modern colour which fits well in a contemporary context, with good examples coming from Sadolin: their Wild Grape is superb in their range of opaque woodstains. Mauve, such as HC87 from

OPPOSITE *Mauve is an unusual but dramatic colour to choose. I designed this garden using predominantly purple and mauves for the foliage and flowers which surround a formal pool. The colour-coordinated fencing reinforces the theme throughout the year. A similar colour is available from Papers & Paints, No. HC 87.*

ABOVE *This blue-grey door combines well the with the more luxuriant planting and the eclectic range of pots to create an area with a bold, rather tropical feel to it. The blue tones also bring a feeling of calm to the scene.*

RIGHT *The blue finish on this dramatic ornately detailed bench allows it to integrate very easily into the garden.*

Papers & Paints, is far less often used, which makes it all the more startling when used well. I applied the intensely saturated tropical blue of Johnstone's Oxford Blue extensively in the Paradise Garden I made for Wyevale Garden Centres at the Chelsea Flower Show in 1996. It certainly injected an exotic flavour to the garden, and reminded me of the wonderful Majorelle Gardens in Marrakesh. I re-used several of these pots in the traditional walled garden of my own centuries-old Cambridgeshire farmhouse, and am always surprised by how good they look. If I had not had them already I would never have thought of choosing the colour from a paint chart!

BLUE

1| A lattice-work gate is enhanced by a pale grey-blue paint finish that tones well with the surrounding plants and creates a strong focal point. **2|** This garden, designed by Keela Meadows, demonstrates how the right blue can effectively pull together disparate elements and bring harmony to a garden. **3|** In some areas Farrow & Ball's Berrington Blue can appear too grey, so I lightened it by mixing it with equal parts of Farrow & Ball's Ballroom Blue for this tree seat. **4|** This small mosaic pool was designed by Ann Frith and coordinates with the cobalt blue walls behind. The well-sited mirror and expanse of blue opens out the small space. **5|** These concrete balls are painted with Oxford Blue emulsion paint, which contrasts with the soft mauve of the path, designed by Bonita

Bulaitis. This strong blue needs careful handling in northern Europe as it can be too dominant under grey skies – use it in small areas well broken up with plants or other elements. **6|** This garden, designed for the Chelsea Flower Show 1997 by Maddison Cox, accurately matches the blue of the Majorelle Gardens in Marrakesh. **7|** Strong, lush planting combined with a repeated use of grey-blue on trelliswork and pots provides a unifying element as well as cool, calm permanent colour. **8|** The pale blue colour used on the shutters of a house in the South of France is repeated throughout the garden. It tones perfectly with the stonework and maintains the historic feel of the property. **9|** This nineteenth-century bench has been painted cornflower blue, which works well on the lattice-work, creating a strong impression without dominating.

Green

Very dark green   *Blue green*   *Olive green*   *Pea green*   *Very pale mint green*   *Verdigris*

Green is extremely restful to the eye and is the predominant colour in most gardens. Yet it is surprisingly difficult to use it on hard surfaces; it often appears intrusive, especially if the shade is too close to that of the planting. Strong contrasting greens often work better, for example, bright yellow greens or darker olive greens. It is understandable why people paint large unattractive structures green, believing that this will help them slip into the background. To achieve this, however, the green would need to be very dark, almost black, before it would recede and take a back seat. To help conceal large timber structures, such as long stretches of panel fencing you could paint the panels with a translucent, very dark green, such as Carolina Stone from Sadolin, which would allow the grain of the timber to show through. Sections of trellis, painted in another very dark green, such as Dark Olive (58.16g39y) made by Jotun, could then be superimposed onto the dark green panels. This would create a textured background of greens which would easily harmonize with the rest of the garden.

Green pigments used to be very expensive and prone to fading, which limited their use. Now, however, modern green paints are very practical and their use in the garden infinite. The colour swatch shows six greens that I use regularly. A good very dark green is Trust Green No. 35, by Farrow & Ball. Although it seems deceptively black against the white of the page and swatch card, it is ideal for knocking back eyesores or for a restrained classic effect. Pea Green No. 33, also by Farrow & Ball, can be brightened further by adding yellow ochre or blue stainers to it. It is a surprisingly adaptable hue provided it is not used in large blocks, as it tends to lift and brighten its surroundings. Green is particularly useful for linking house and garden, and Lichen No. 19, a soft green by Farrow & Ball, or Jungle Green from Sadolin's Superdec range, are ideal for painting on doors, windows and conservatories, where they will associate well with climbers and shrubs and complement any stonework, as will the subtle tones of HC72, William and Mary Green by Papers & Paints. True verdigris is a natural patina which forms on copper, and as such varies tremendously, but the soft, light tones of Verdigris No. 14, from Fired Earth's 'Historic Colours', are especially effective for highlighting small features.

A deep blue-green such as Cotton Blue HC16 by Papers & Paints looks particularly good against purple flowers, but it is best avoided near yellow-green foliage. The very pale mint green of Clover Leaf, from Sadolin's Superdec range (see the gypsy caravan on page 89) is another favourite; it combines well with gilt and dark reds, and small dashes of it here and there lighten the overall look. It is worth considering shifting the tones on a large vertical structure. When I painted my children's treehouse I put a dark green near the base, which was in shadow, and gradually lightened the green as I reached the top and the bigger pools of sunlight. This effect is suitable for any vertical structure set among planting, although I would avoid it for large, exposed, solid areas.

BELOW *The bold light pea green used on this conservatory gives a fresh, bright character to the space and tones well with the bright green of the foliage of* Abutilon.

GREEN

1| The doors and tree seat on this garden building, which I designed for a small London garden, have been painted with Farrow & Ball's Trust Green No. 35. It is an excellent very dark green which enhances the mirrored panels in the door. The remainder of the building was painted with a translucent woodstain, Carolina Stone, by Sadolin. **2|** In this 'Herbalist's Garden' which I designed on behalf of Wyevale Garden Centres for the Chelsea Flower Show 1998, I chose a bright pea green stained finish for the timber posts to freshen up and enhance the predominantly green feel provided by the many different herbs. **3|** This door in the garden of the stonemason Bas Clarke is painted in Farrow & Ball's Calke Green – a colour based on the Breakfast Room at Calke Abbey – which works well with brick and stone. **4|** On another Chelsea garden, which I designed for Wyevale Garden Centres in 1996, I contrasted the pale verdigris finish of the tree house balustrade (similar to Sadolin's Clover Leaf) with the warm Tuscan pink render (similar to Ointment Pink from Farrow & Ball) of the walls. **5|** The strong blue-green paint finish on the arch sets off the vivid pale mauve of the plants in the foreground, illustrating how effective coloured hard surfaces can be when used thoughtfully with organic garden colour. **6|** Here, garden designer George Carter has added some structure to an informal border by erecting some timber wigwams stained in an olive green. These act as 'punctuation points', giving definition to the border.

Red

Bright red   *Strawberry pink*   *Warm pink*   *Terracotta*   *Dark brick red*

Red can evoke a wide range of emotions and can mean quite different things in different cultures. For some it symbolizes love and passion, for others fire or danger, and others still find it hot and exciting. A cooler effect can be achieved by mixing the red of your choice with white. Surprisingly enough, it is an excellent colour to splash in the landscape, as it works equally well with earth and rocks as it does with the greens of plants. In the eighteenth century it was used extensively on iron bridges; the red lead oxide not only protected the metal but also made an attractive contrast to the dark water running below.

The colour swatch shows five reds that I recommend. Bright reds, such as Johnstone's Paints Post Office Red, can be strident, making objects jump forward and dominate. This is why, of course, telephone kiosks and pillar boxes are painted scarlet in some countries. Like blues and greens, saturated reds are difficult to handle across large areas, but are pleasantly striking on pergola beams or smaller decorative items where they impart a strong oriental feel. Some reds, such as strawberry pink, feel warmer and brighter, for example the intense but subtle Famille Rose HC133 from Papers & Paints, and the traditional warm Suffolk pink, such as Dulux's 1220-Y82R. It is called Suffolk pink because it captures the qualities of the pink used in the villages of Suffolk, England, where it bestows a cosy, welcoming identity on the local landscape.

Dark brick reds, such as Eating Room Red No. 43 by Farrow & Ball and Papers & Paints' HC106, are excellent colours for use on finials, posts or doorways, perhaps used in contrast with pale greens. They combine well with brick, stone and timber. They became popular in England in Victorian times and, although often associated with rather rich, heavy interiors, can look striking when used outdoors on gates, furniture, lighting columns or bridges. Dark reds also contrast strikingly with pale grey-blues and greens and work particularly well on fences, where the posts can take the chosen blue or green hue with dark red giving a flourish to the finials.

The soft, earthy hues of terracotta pink suggested by Aubusson Red HC123 by Papers & Paints also combines well with brick, stone and timber. Terracotta ranges from the strong orange tones traditional in Spain to the pale chalky pink of some Greek potteries. When combining the colour with natural stone, I usually favour the latter. To soften the former, which tends to tone down over a few seasons anyway, you can 'age' it either with a warm pink masonry paint (such as Farrow & Ball's Ointment Pink) or by rubbing dock leaves and soil over certain areas, particularly nearer the base where it is damper. This colour also works well on rendered walls, combining pleasingly with brickwork and stone.

BELOW *This eye-catching area of colour is formed in polished plaster and is an exciting blood red, contrasting with the cool neutral colour that surrounds it. It was designed by Christopher Bradley-Hole in a Chelsea Flower Show garden sponsored by the* Daily Telegraph.

RED

1| This eye-catching area of colour is formed from rendered concrete block work that has been transformed by a bright but earthy colour that looks well with the various red tones used in the planting. The colour is similar to the dark brick red used in the swatch on page 18. **2|** This Wendy house in my own garden is fairly discreetly hidden at the end of some pleached hornbeams. In order to make you aware that there is something there, the front door and shutters have been picked out in bright red to make them stand out. **3|** The splashes of this unusual strawberry pink, as shown in the swatch on page 18, serve to enhance the building's individual style and give it added warmth and strength. **4|** This Sienna pink render is one of a palette of about 60 colours used to great effect in Portmeirion in Wales. Small splashes of Portmeirion Green (their own secret recipe) are repeatedly introduced for contrast and continuity. The base colour is subtly lightened on the buildings with white as the painter works up the building to highlight the tone. **5|** The application of an unusual colour and simple heart-shaped cut-out transforms this door into a distinctive feature. The pinky red is similar to HC133 from Papers & Paints. **6|** This dark, pinky brown, another Portmeirion colour, increases the Italianate feel of the architecture. Keim masonry paints are used throughout the village on the rendered surfaces. **7|** Here I've painted the terracotta pots with Ointment Pink masonry paint from Farrow & Ball to tone down the pot for use against stonework.

Yellow

Saturated yellow   *Soft lemon yellow*   *Buff yellow*   *Bamboo yellow*

Yellow is my favourite colour. When saturated it is highly reflective and therefore easily seen. It has a spreading effect, the opposite of red, which tends to contract and pull things together. Yellow is at its brightest when it is fully saturated, unlike most colours which become slightly darker when fully saturated. However, it is quite overwhelming in this form, especially if it is put next to stone or brick. (In the Georgian town of Bath, in Somerset, England, the local planning department obtained permission to modify the standard bold shade of yellow used for road markings to a softer tone which would associate better with the warm honey-coloured local stone.) However, small dashes of it in the garden make brilliant punctuations against foliage green. Persian Yellow HC15 from Papers & Paints is a strong yellow that is very effective, especially in warm climates.

Yellow is a rewarding colour and I particularly enjoy using the four colours in the colour swatch. The pale buff hues of Farrow & Ball's Gervase Yellow are ideal for blending in with plants. Architectural features, doors, pots and backdrop walls are also flatteringly highlighted by these tones. A bamboo yellow such as Straw Colour SC209 from Papers & Paints is a useful colour, suitable for mellowing large areas.

The soft lemon yellows, such as Aconite Yellow No. 20 from Fired Earth, are fun colours to incorporate, and contrast well with pale blues, dark greens and maroons.

RIGHT *The gentle tones of this warm yellow with pink tones work well in the north European light yet also evoke a feel of warmer climes. The yellow is enhanced by the contrasting turquoise blue seat.*

YELLOW

1| The saturated yellow on this simple garden chair draws out the yellow tones of the fennel behind. A moveable object like a chair is ideal for experimenting with more challenging colours as it can be shifted or put away as the flowering or light quality changes. **2|** A gentle buff yellow has been painted onto a mortar wall to set off lush green herb plantings. It also complements the terracotta of the containers and tiled surface. Buff yellow is an easy colour to live with on a regular basis and therefore ideally suited to an area near to the house that you use a lot – a terraced eating area, for example. **3|** Here the architect/landscape architect Michael Balston has chosen a buff yellow to enhance this single-storey building. The yellow combines well with the bleached oak colour of the conservatory, enhancing the qualities of both. **4|** Saturated yellows are

difficult to use in parts of the world more accustomed to grey skies than blue but when applied in small bands such as on this gate they can provide that extra inspirational boldness wherever you live. **5|** A bamboo yellow wash, a small shelf and fragrant honeysuckles all help to transform this wall into a delightfully informal but eye-catching focal point that forms an interesting backdrop to the garden. The design is by Mirabel Osler. **6|** A carefully thought out paint colour applied to an acorn finial transforms a simple white rendered concrete retaining wall to enhance some steps at Portmeirion. These acorn finials, as well as many other shapes, are available in terracotta from C.H. Brannam Ltd (see Suppliers' Guide). Failing this, Whichford Potteries will make finials to order (see Suppliers' Guide). The terracotta can then be painted in any colour of your choice.

Rustic shades

Bleached oak

Walnut

Butterscotch

Gingerbread

Red/brown

Rustic colours, by which I mean the browns, rusts and beiges associated with wood and timber, have been used for centuries in the garden environment. They harmonize perfectly with the natural greens of foliage, and occur naturally whenever untreated timber is used. They blend well with brick, stone and gravel, thereby forming the perfect link between garden and house.

The danger is perhaps that because they are so easy to use these colours have become somewhat over familiar, and we are a bit blasé about them. However, by emphasizing their particular qualities it becomes possible to make a stronger statement.

If I am aiming for a rustic effect, I may want to emphasize all the nobbles and organic shapes of wood, so I tend to leave timber structures unpainted, to weather and bleach naturally over a few seasons. The same effect can be achieved more speedily by painting any timber structure with a turpentine linseed mix such as John Brown's recipe (see page 34), which will give an instantly more weathered, greyer finish.

When I specify more elaborate timber structures, such as pergolas or archways or buildings, I tend to finish them with a rustic stain such as Sadolin's Gingerbread, or no.4 Walnut from Trebitt/Oxan WP. The strong yellow hue of butterscotch imparts a bold, modern look to structures, whereas gingerbread harmonizes with most tones of brickwork. Translucent and opaque woodstains are widely available from most paint manufacturers in most rustic colours. Rustic colours can be applied to surfaces other than timber, such as the rendered surface of the piers shown in the photograph below – the colour imparts an organic feel to the man-made material. Deep red/brown ochres are often used for tinting limewashes.

1| This beautifully detailed doorway with its bleached oak door is at The Old Vicarage, East Ruston. Oak will fade to this colour naturally in quite a short space of time. **2|** This see-through door entices you into the next garden room. The timber colour has the appearance of a walnut tone (see swatch above). **3|** This eye-catching obelisk is made of oak but has been painted with linseed oil, which gives it a warm butterscotch colour. **4|** The gingerbread colour on these piers defines the gateway and works well with the surrounding organic hues.

Neutral shades

Pale beige

Pale grey

Grey lilac

Off-white

Stone

Neutral stone shades such as Farrow & Ball's London Stone No. 6 are an essential part of hard garden colour. They are often used to make rendered walls, concrete, or even timber look like stone. The late David Hicks, for instance, painted large plastic flowerpots in a stone colour for his garden with a very convincing result. In the same garden, I coveted some splendid 'stone' finials on huge stone piers that were made from marine plywood, painted with a couple of coats of stone-coloured emulsion: certainly a kinder option to one's bank balance than their stone equivalents would have been. (If you are trying to create a sandstone effect on a rendered building, as an alternative to applying a layer of paint you could use a pale-coloured sand in the render, leaving the surface unpainted. This is convincingly textural and has the added advantage of saving on maintenance.)

I occasionally use neutral shades for finials; their paleness makes them stand out within the planting context and they also contrast well with many darker colours. If you want to diminish the impact of high-level finials that might be too dominant if not carefully handled, a neutral colour knocks them back allowing them to harmonize with the sky, as for example Farrow & Ball's String No. 8.

A more original neutral colour is the blue-grey of the shutters shown below in the photograph, which can be achieved with a translucent woodstain such as Sadolin's Classic Satin Lilac.

1| Here the finials which I used to emphasize the bird theme in a garden for the elderly at the Chelsea Flower Show 1997 are highlighted with the neutral colour String No. 8, from Farrow & Ball. **2|** This grey-lilac is an unusual and subtle colour for all the woodwork on Anna Simond's French farmhouse. **3|** Greys are a useful range of colours for the garden as they have an organic appearance and so work well with many building materials. Here these false doors are painted a soft, pale grey and form a focal point at the top of a cascade. **4|** The woodwork on this orangery designed by architect Robert Weighton is finished in an off-white shade. A good off-white is BS 10B15. **5|** These pots have been painted with London Stone No. 6 from Farrow & Ball.

Black & white

Black and white are not always considered colours in their own right because of their light absorption and reflection qualities. Carbon black will absorb 97% of light while a bright magnesium oxide white will reflect about 98% of light, so absolute shades of either are avoided altogether on colour charts. Nonetheless, for gardening and landscaping purposes different tones of these colours are very useful. White is traditional and used to be very commonly used mainly because it was readily made by grinding chalk and limestone rocks into powder and then mixing them with milk or size. Brilliant white paint, on the other hand, was not available until the mid-twentieth century, so discerning architects often specify a soft creamier white for properties which pre-date this period. Today, white continues to have a crisp summery feel resonant of the striped lawns and cricket pavilions of England. On a practical note, white is visible over long distances, and is therefore a good colour to choose for objects which you want to draw attention to. It also reflects heat effectively.

Black is a good colour for camouflaging eyesores (see also very dark green, page 16). It has the opposite effect to white, and makes surfaces recede. However, its use is not only limited to counteracting negative impacts. Garden designer Cleve West, in his small London garden, has stained his timber pergola an opaque black, and almost totally surrounded it with lush greens of plantings. The effect is very calm and contemporary.

1| White stands out and pulls the eye towards it. This well-detailed trellis deserves attention and furthermore acts as a clean backdrop for the bold pinks, purples and greens, giving them greater impact too. 2| This doorway, designed by Lanning Roper, deserves the attention the white ensures it receives. The columns and the simple yet elegant trellis doorway are softened and anchored by the heavy planting above. 3| In the white garden at Woolerton Old Hall in Shropshire, the restricted palette of green, white and black creates a calm, bold and sophisticated feel, and illustrates how colour dictates mood. 4| Here the black emphasizes the shape of the arbour, adds a feeling of distance and looks very smart. It contrasts with the brilliant spots of red from the beans and geraniums.

Metallic colours

Gold invariably produces a spectacular finish but with the vast range of 'fake' finishes available on the market it requires careful handling to deliver the punch. Historically, gold and other precious metals have always been highly prized and regarded as a sign of ostentation and grandeur and our sense of wonder at the sight of well-executed metallic finishes is partly due to our association with these characteristics. Gold in particular is incomparable if you are looking for a theatrical feel, and gold leaf is the best way of achieving a permanent finish, although it is expensive and takes time to apply. For external work, a high-carat gold such as 23.5–24 carat must be used, as the red and yellow golds oxidize more and so are not suitable. Buy the books containing 25 sheets of transfer gold leaf on wax-backed paper – it is extremely difficult to use ordinary gold leaf outside because it blows away! You can apply gold leaf to virtually any surface as long as you prime it first with an oil-based primer followed by an oil gold size. Silver, gold, copper and other metallic colours are often considered alien in a garden environment. However, modern properties with an abundance of reflective materials such as mirrors, glass and metal may benefit from the link that the colours will provide between house and garden.

1| A garden is an ideal place to introduce some fun and a spectacular finial like this is well worth the thought and effort required. The colours are reminiscent of Chinese pagodas or perhaps Russian Orthodox Church onion domes, and the gold finish is the icing on the cake. **2|** This gate at The Old Vicarage, East Ruston, created by Alan Gray and Graham Robeson, forms an enchanting entrance and the addition of gold leaf to the finials lifts their appearance immeasurably. About two and a half books of gold leaf were used. Visitors to the garden find the finials irresistible to touch, and if they have long nails tend to leave scratch marks – so be warned. **3|** This sculptural 'fence' was designed by Peter Styles. The timber columns have been sprayed with an aerosol red-gold metallic spray, and they are topped off with timber cubes painted Oxford Blue. **4|** A fake lead finish has been applied to this fencepost and finial which makes it look quite old. In fact the spherical finial is a reclaimed ballcock and therefore wholly modern – see page 42 for fake lead techniques.

paint
techniques

THE WIDE VARIETY OF PAINTS AND WOODSTAINS ON THE MARKET TODAY PROVIDE THE ESSENTIAL INGREDIENTS FOR BOTH SIMPLE USES OF COLOUR IN THE GARDEN AND MORE ELABORATE PAINT FINISHES. STARTING WITH VARIATIONS ON FLAT COLOUR ACHIEVED BY FINISHES SUCH AS LIME-WASH AND ENDING WITH MORE ELABO-RATE TECHNIQUES SUCH AS TROMPE L'OEIL AND FAKE LEAD METHODS, THIS CHAPTER REVEALS THE WIDE RANGE OF MAGICAL TRANSFORMATIONS THAT CAN BE ACHIEVED BY MANIPULATING PAINT. WORKMANLIKE SURFACES SUCH AS CONCRETE RENDER CAN BE TRANS-FORMED TO LOOK LIKE TIME-WORN STONEWORK BY PAINTING IN WALL LINES AND SHADING BLOCKS OF 'STONE', WHILE VERDIGRIS, LEAD AND GOLD EFFECTS CAN DISGUISE PLASTIC, TERRA-COTTA AND WOOD.

New paint finishes

BELOW LEFT *A vibrant blue woodstain used on cantilevered timber steps challenges the conventional organic approach.*

BELOW RIGHT *Far from playing down its functional finish, the owners chose a bold masonry paint to make this wall an integral part of the garden.*

WOODSTAINS

In the last 10 years or so woodstains have become available in a huge array of colours, and although many builders' merchants only display a few shades, if you contact the manufacturers you will often find a superb range is available (see Supplier's Guide). Some firms will even colour match any shade for you.

Opaque woodstains, to all intents and purposes, look like paint and no wood grain will show through at all. Translucent woodstains, on the other hand, highlight the grain of the wood, and can provide more or less depth of colour according to the number of coats you apply. The great advantages of stains over traditional paint are that they are much easier to apply than a gloss paint, they are quick drying, they give protection to the wood

and, when you have to repaint, they do not need much surface preparation. They are available in a matt or gloss finish.

MASONRY PAINTS

External walls, whether they are stone, concrete rendered or brick, are usually painted with an exterior masonry paint, which is available in a smooth or textured finish. These paints come in a large range of colours, including historic ones, and have a number of properties which make them particularly suitable for external use, such as the inclusion of fungicides and algicides to inhibit mould growth. They are also colour fast. You can alter the texture a little yourself by the addition of sand.

LIMEWASH

Limewash is a wonderful, soft, powdery finish that can be tinted by adding universal stainers or bought already tinted in a fantastic range of organic colours (see Supplier's Guide). It has been used for centuries, and it is often seen on buildings where it has been mixed with local earth pigments.

Limewash is ideal to use on most porous surfaces, and gives a mellow finish that begins by being slightly translucent but once the full number of layers are applied becomes quite opaque. It is never totally uniform and it also weathers unevenly, which is all part of its charm. It has the big advantage of allowing moisture

to pass through so rising damp can escape, whereas masonry paint is impermeable, allowing moisture to build up behind it to lift the finish off.

To Make Limewash

Although it is available ready-made from paint suppliers, you can easily make limewash at home: just take one part of lime putty and mix with two parts of water to create a watery thin liquid. If the surface is going to be exposed to extreme weather conditions, add binders such as tallow, casein or linseed oil (see Suppliers' Guide) to the limewash to increase its binding capacity. Apply several coats, maybe as many as six, waiting for each to dry for at least 24 hours before applying the next one. Protect from rain and bright sunlight during the drying period. (If limewash dries too quickly it cannot absorb enough carbon dioxide and tends to flake.) Lime is caustic, so be sure to wear skin and eye protection when you are working.

To Make Coloured Limewash

For the colour, use pure pigments (in the form of universal stainers) which are compatible with lime, such as yellow ochre, burnt umber, red ochre or cobalt.

Ultramarine is adversely affected by lime and has to be applied after mixing. It might be a good idea to paint small trial areas and speed-dry them with a hair dryer to get a better idea of the finished effect.

Application of Limewash

Note that limewash carbonates when exposed to air, returning to its original calcium carbonate state. This means white becomes brighter and colours more enhanced over long periods of time. This carbonation carries on indefinitely, so when you repaint do not remove previous coats but simply apply new ones.

Limewash is especially successful when used on freshly applied lime render or plaster, but it also works well on weathered Portland cement and gypsum plaster. Bricks are fine if they are dampened prior to coating; however, because they are very porous they will require several coats.

Timber boarding can be imbued with an air of permanence by the application of a traditional finish of limewash, though it may be necessary to add tallow or linseed oil to the mixture to get it to bond. Limewash producers will often make up a special mix for a particular situation.

RIGHT *Limewashed pots. These previously bright orange terracotta pots jarred against the Cotswold stone of the building and so a limewash mix was applied to provide a paler finish. Humphry Repton used this technique in the eighteenth century.*

Plaster & render effects

There are several traditional plaster and render finishes which offer ranges of colour and texture. They enable you to ring the changes and make a feature of a blank gable end wall, for example.

STUCCO

Stucco is a carefully detailed and precise finish which results in a hard-wearing, fine-textured plaster typically associated with elegant Georgian town houses in England. It is often applied to imitate coursed, dressed stonework, a skill developed by the Romans thousands of years ago. As many as 12 coats may be applied, the final one formed from marble dust and slaked lime to give it its very regular finish.

Marmorino is a type of stucco which can be coloured by adding either marble dust or pigments to it. It has a fabulously smooth finish and is equally suitable for use with traditional elements in a garden or with high-tech modern materials such as stainless steel, glass and concrete. Both marmorino and ordinary stucco are highly specialized finishes and are best left to professionals.

ROUGH PLASTER

To contrast with the perfect finish of the stucco, rough plastering using a coarse 'haired' lime plaster has a highly uneven finish which creates shadows on the surface, thereby adding depth to colour. It is often finished with a limewash, but can be left natural or painted.

LIME RENDER

A lime render, usually applied in two coats, using lime putty and coarse sand in a ratio of 1:4, can provide a stunning self-coloured surface, which can be varied depending on the colour of sand used. If you are combining it with natural stone, using the stone to pick up details such as quoins on corners, buttresses or coping, match the colour of the render to the stone to create the feel of a convincing stone mass.

RIGHT *Dark blue stained doors are surrounded by a marmarino render. John Harvey Simpson has decorated the pale yellow finish with a watercolour motif. He is also responsible for the stained glass in the door. They were part of Fiona Lawrenson's garden for Sky Television at the Chelsea Flower Show 1998.*

FAR RIGHT (ABOVE) *A rough plaster finish enhances these walls designed by Fiona Lawrenson. For a Chelsea Flower Show garden, they look extremely established even though they have only been installed for about 20 days. The rough plaster was applied to block work in three layers, and in conjunction with the colour wash (by John Harvey Simpson) immediately imparts a feeling of age.*

FAR RIGHT (BELOW) *The newly built Orangery at Elton Hall, Northamptonshire, has a warm, stone-coloured render finish which works well with the reconstituted stone elements. The colour of the sand in the render contributes to the finished result.*

INCORPORATING MOTIFS INTO RENDER

To add another dimension you can apply simple motifs to the surface of render. Either buy ready-made moulds and fill them with a 1:5 cement/sand mix, or use actual shells, pebbles and ammonites and attach them to the surface with more wet render.

PEBBLEDASH

A pebbledash finish can be achieved by incorporating a chipping of the desired colour into the final layer of render. Although this finish has been overused in an unsympathetic way in modern housing, it can work well in a garden situation. It is formed by liberally throwing suitable chipping (choose what you like at a builders' merchant) onto the wet render until you achieve the desired coating.

IMITATION STONEWORK

In the eighteenth century it was the fashion to simulate stone blocks on the exterior of buildings by painting lines on plain plaster walls. These wall lines have recently become very popular for modern interiors. In the garden, the illusion created by wall lines is easy to create, partly because you usually start with a textured surface, and partly because plants deflect the eye from examining details too closely. A well-planted border in front of the wall makes close inspection even less likely.

To paint wall lines

The choice of colour and texture of the background surface is very important. If there is any real stone in close proximity obviously be guided by this. In the example overleaf, the existing render was extremely textured and would not have formed a convincing background for the stone finish that we were aiming for, so I asked a contractor to apply a smoother sand-and-cement render to the surface before we started work. I wanted a finish that resembled a wall built of ashlar stone, so after the smooth render had dried we applied a stone-coloured masonry paint. Bearing in mind we were going to apply a colour wash over much of the base, the choice of colour needed to be neutral stone but was not too critical. Next we pencilled in the lines of the courses of stonework using the edge of a spirit level as a guide and lightly scored the render. The size of the stone blocks and style of coursing should conform roughly to any used nearby.

Then a colour wash using acrylic paints and masonry paint was applied. The acrylic colours used were sap green, raw umber, black and yellow ochre. These were put in a paint rolling tray in distinct 'blobs' using two parts each of the sap green, black and raw umber and one part of the yellow ochre. Water with 10% PVA (to help fix the paint) was then added to form a translucent, watery wash. The trick is not to mix the colours completely but to have distinct areas of different shades in your tray so that you can apply different ranges of tone all over the wall. The wash was applied over the surface with a paint brush in a quick, quite haphazard way. One in every six blocks was painted more carefully with a slightly less watery wash to make it look especially convincing. You could paint every block if you have time.

Finally, we painted the joints using a very fine brush loaded with masonry paint which had been mixed with black emulsion to form a dark grey colour. All the joints were finely picked out in this colour. On this particular wall the sunlight comes predominantly from the south (that is to say from the left-hand side on the photographs), so a thin line was painted in a lighter masonry paint immediately to the right of the darker joint line to simulate the effect of the sun. Similarly, where small cracks and crevices were painted on a block, small highlights were painted immediately to the right of them.

Wall lines

Painting wall lines on a rendered wall

This simple method involves etching out fake joints in a render to give the appearance of stone blocks. It is necessary to do it when the render is not quite dry, and so involves getting a contractor to apply a thin external sand and cement render to the wall. If this is not feasible, painting the lines still gives a good effect.

Materials

Masonry paint
Acrylic paints: sap green, raw umber and yellow ochre
PVA
Water
Black emulsion
Fine paintbrush
Large paintbrush
Roller tray

1| *After the wall has been rendered but before the render has fully hardened off, use a pencil and spirit level to mark out the 'stone blocks' which represent the corner quoins.*

2| *Draw a bolster or chisel along the edge of a spirit level (or other straight edge) and lightly score the still slightly soft render along the pencil lines to create the illusion of joints around the corner quoins.*

3| *Apply a masonry paint to the whole rendered area. A light stone-coloured smooth-textured paint was chosen in this case. Then use a spirit level to mark out the lines in pencil which are to form the fake joints in the rest of the stonework.*

4| *Fill a roller tray with blobs of sap green, raw umber and yellow ochre acrylic paints in proportions of 2:2:1, add water with 10% PVA to form a translucent wash and paint over the wall, mixing different shades and proportions as you go to give a stone wash.*

5| *When the colour wash has dried (this will be quick), paint the joints and cracks using the masonry paint as a base tinted down to a dark grey with black emulsion.*

6| *Using a natural sponge, pick out a few blocks and using a less watered down wash paint them individually in slightly differing tones.*

7| *Use a fine paintbrush and a straight edge if necessary to add highlights to the right-hand side of the darker joints to mimic the shadows caused by sunlight coming from the left-hand side of the picture and catching the top edge of the blocks.*

RIGHT *To add further interest, a simple trompe l'oeil was painted at a suitable point within the stone-blocked wall. (See page 39 for step-by-step instructions.)*

Distressing & ageing

Ideal for giving a soft, weathered patina to new wood and paintwork, distressing techniques help to create the illusion of permanence in a garden, imbuing it with a gentle faded charm.

OAK AND MAHOGANY

Lime water, which forms on the top of limewash when it is left to stand, is the ideal medium to use if you want to age some new oak or mahogany in the garden and give it a weathered look. Simply paint it on and it will react with the tannic acid in these particular woods, instantly forming a well-worn look.

JOHN BROWN'S RECIPE

John Brown's recipe is a good mixture for ageing new pine and other timbers. It is a simple, inexpensive mixture, both to make and to use. Mix equal parts of turpentine substitute and boiled linseed oil with a dash of white oil paint. (For 600ml [1 pint] of linseed and white spirit, use ½ cup of paint). Put them in a large bottle, shake well and then apply to the surface with a rag or brush. This is not a precise recipe – you can adapt it to your needs. For a good bleached oaky colour, add a minute quantity of brown and black oil stainers to the mixture. If you want to achieve a hint of green or blue, substitute the appropriate coloured stainers. Disperse the colours well by mixing them in gradually and thoroughly agitate them before adding the rest.

External timber will need to be treated every two or so years. However, when you are repainting use the oil and white spirit mix without the paint or stainers in order to avoid a build-up of colour.

PAINT-ON-PAINT FINISH

This is an extremely simple technique that gives painted timber a well-weathered character, making it look delightfully faded and battered. In addition to helping the garden look as though it has been established for some time, this technique also helps to break up solid blocks of colour so that they blend in well with their surroundings.

Good Colour Combinations

Some successful colour schemes I have used for distressing have been a pale minty green applied over a dark red to give the appearance of verdigris. On another occasion I used cornflower blue applied over white for

some louvred doors to a garden building. This helped soften what would otherwise have been a solid, rather obtrusive mass of blue. Deep reds can be toned down by olive green, and then heavily rubbed to reveal almost half the red again. Bright pea greens can be used over sienna browns to reduce their vibrance. If you do not like the effect you get, you can always paint over it with something else and start again. But before you make any rash decisions, live with the finished product for a bit and observe it at different times of the day and under varying weather conditions.

Choice of Paint

For external timber work oil-based paints are recommended. It is easier to rub the paint back with thinned oil-based paints, using white spirit as a thinner for the top coat. If you are applying more than two coats, progressively thin down the subsequent coats.

When you have applied the first coat of paint, let it dry and then apply some wax over the surface using a candle. The subsequent layers of paint will not adhere very well to the areas coated by wax, and they will be easier to expose. A genuinely well-worn door is usually most bare around the handle and any part of it which stands proud, so apply your wax particularly to these areas. Next paint the following slightly thinned coat of paint in a contrasting colour. When it is dry gently rub the paint back using a sanding block until you achieve a convincing surface.

ABOVE This wavy gate in my garden leads on to a cornfield. It has just been made from new pine. In order to give it the appearance of bleached oak (ABOVE RIGHT) I have applied some of John Brown's recipe with an old rag. It is a quick finish to apply and can be treated annually.

RIGHT *These false louvred doors in a trellis boundary fence add interest to this tiny space. The distressed powder blue paint finish calms down the predominantly white planting.*

Paint Distressing a Garden Door

This illustrates how to create a distressed paint finish for a garden door. The method has been kept very simple, using only two colours to create a subtle effect. If you wish for a more elaborate finish, add additional coats and bring in more colours. The hinges are painted on for decoration.

Materials

Primer
Undercoat
Paint in two contrasting colours
White spirit for thinning
Wax candle
Sanding block

1| *Make sure the surface to be painted is clean and dry, and apply a primer and undercoat. Once they are dry apply your first colour. Here I used Farrow & Ball's Picture Gallery Red No. 42.*

2| *Ensure the first coat is quite dry and then apply the wax to the areas which you wish to expose. Put the candle on its side and roll it over the paint so the wax highlights the pattern of the wood grain. Concentrate on areas which wear naturally, such as around the handle or on the edges of raised panels.*

3| *Apply your next coat of contrasting colour. I have used Farrow & Ball's Green Smoke No. 47, thinned by adding 30% white spirit to make the rubbing back easier.*

4| *Once the paint is dry, rub back the surface using a sanding block. The top coat will come off fairly easily where the wax has been applied. At intervals, stand back and examine the overall effect. Do not worry if you have taken too much off, as it will not take long to paint over where required.*

Trompe l'oeil

If you wish to incorporate fun and interest into a small space, a well-sited trompe l'oeil may be the answer. The drawback is that unless you can paint it yourself, an original trompe l'oeil can be very expensive. A cheaper alternative suitable for the interior of garden buildings is a technique called oleography. It involves photographically reproducing a trompe l'oeil onto marine plywood and then hand finishing it to make it look authentic (see Suppliers' Guide for details).

One of the most important factors to bear in mind is the siting of a trompe l'oeil. They only work successfully when viewed from a certain position because the perspective, highlights and shadows are obviously only two-dimensional, so put your trompe l'oeil somewhere where you cannot get too close to it and where it will be viewed from a single location.

The control of light is also very important. If, for example, the sun is casting shadows in the opposite direction to the painted shadow the whole thing will look pretty odd, so if you are relying on natural light always place a trompe l'oeil on a north wall or on one that does not receive direct sunlight.

RIGHT *This garden, designed by Mike Miller of Clifton Nurseries, includes a pair of blue doors with mirrors in them to give the illusion that they lead on to another space.*

FAR RIGHT *This dramatic trompe l'oeil was painted by Martin Rodgers (see Suppliers' Guide) which I designed for the Herbalist's Garden for the Chelsea Flower Show 1998. It was used to make the garden building (in reality a cupboard) look bigger and was heavily lit in order for it to stand out. The dragon hinges were made by Fotheringhay forge.*

RIGHT *This bold but cohesive garden is given an extra dimension by the addition of the trompe l'oeil by Francis Hamel-Cooke. The inclusion of the framework is a simple but useful way to give it the necessary emphasis.*

Painting a Trompe l'Oeil

It is, of course, possible to paint simple trompe l'oeils yourself, perhaps formed in conjunction with trellis against a wall. If you follow some basic rules it is possible, if you are reasonably good at painting, to get a realistic result. If you have had little or no experience of painting, choose a simple subject matter, such as an urn in a niche or an obelisk. Create the shadow patterns where they would fall naturally with the prevailing light conditions.

Materials

Acrylic paints

Paintbrushes

Old paint can (to draw around)

1| *The rendered wall had been painted with a stone-coloured masonry paint, and is in a fairly shaded garden, where the sunlight comes predominantly from the southwest. A simple alcove was outlined in pencil with a straight-edge ledge using an old paint can with a raised handle to form the arch.*

2| *The flower pot and plant were then pencilled in and painted on with acrylic paints mixed with 10% PVA. Light from a source at the top left-hand side falling on the round shapes would hit the central portions of the plant and pot and leave the remainder in shadow to various degrees. A thin black line to the right-hand side of the pot and plant differentiates the plant from the alcove, making it stand out.*

3| *The trompe l'oeil looks convincing partly because it is so simple but also because of the accurately painted shadow. With the wall lines, it makes a stunning transformation of a dull rendered wall.*

Sponging

A technique that I find endlessly useful in the garden is sponging. The great value of it is that it breaks up a flat, hard mass of colour, creating a surface with depth to it. It can transform a flat, boring, rendered wall, giving it texture and interest. Conversely, it can help an uneven wall look more uniform.

This is a simple technique to do oneself. The base coat may be matt oil-based paint, emulsion or masonry paint. The last two will soak up some of the super-imposed colours, giving a less defined, more muted appearance, whereas a matt oil-based paint does not absorb subsequent layers. The subsequent layers may be matt oil-based paint which has been thinned with white spirit, masonry paint, or emulsion diluted with water.

Use more than one additional colour to apply to the base colour if you want a more accentuated effect. Alternatively, use just one additional colour and thin it down to get a less differentiated effect. When using two colours, balance how you apply them so that you can still see the base and also so that the mix of the two is consistent throughout.

The type of sponge used affects the pattern, and a natural sponge gives a more random look than a synthetic one. If you do use the latter you have to nibble bits out of it to get an irregular look, which is trickier than it sounds. As you use the sponge, wring it out regularly (in white spirit if using oil-based paint, otherwise in water) to prevent the pores clogging up and destroying the pattern. If you are not happy with the final effect, reapply the base coat and start again.

Another way to break up the harshness of a new paint or terracotta finish, which also ages the subject instantly, is to apply a green wash that gives the impression that algae and lichen have become established. There are different methods, each achieving a slightly different finish. You can rub rhubarb leaves over a surface to leave an instant naturally greened look (any soft leaf in plentiful supply would work). Another method is to smear the surface with wet soil in very small amounts to get a browny tone mixed with the green. Finally, you can blend grass and water and then filter the mixture through a kitchen sieve to get a rich green liquid that you can paint on. These finishes are not permanent, but as they fade natural weathering takes their place.

SPONGING A TERRACOTTA POT

This project illustrates two different ways of sponging a terracotta pot. The first uses two completely different colours, while the second uses two different intensities of one colour. Emulsion paints are not generally recommended for external use, but I have found that they do wear well on terracotta, plastic and reconstituted stone pots. My father used to paint sharks and other sea monsters on our swimming pool walls with multi-coloured emulsions and no protective varnishes, and they (unfortunately for timid bathers) invariably lasted for several seasons, even when covered with chlorinated water.

Materials

Terracotta pot
Base coat paint
Top coat paint
Paintbrush
Natural sponge
White spirit (if using oil-based paint)

1| Make sure the surface of the pot is clean and dry and then brush on the first coat. The colour I used here is Farrow & Ball's Parma Gray No. 27.

2| Using a natural sponge which has been lightly dampened, apply some deeper coloured paint. In this case, I applied Farrow & Ball's Chinese Blue No. 90. In order to create an even look it is necessary to experiment a little, and then, having established your intensity of coverage, try to maintain it.

3| The finished effect has an interesting mottled appearance that associates well with deep blue plants.

1| *A terracotta pot was painted with Farrow & Ball's London Stone No.6 and left to dry. A slightly darker version of the same emulsion was made by mixing in a little black and then sponged on top.*

2| *The finished result shows the subtlety that can be achieved by using different shades of the same paint. The closer the layers of paint are in terms of hue, the less contrived the effect.*

Note:
To protect against frost, apply a coat of masonry paint to the dry surface before primer (or bring inside during winter).

Lead & verdigris

ABOVE *This half container with a fake lead finish was piled up with painted scallop shells and surrounded by mussel shells. Designed by George Carter, it forms a dramatic water feature in the London garden of photographer Marianne Majerus.*

LEAD

Lead is an attractive material for the garden which associates well with most plants and architectural styles. Solid lead containers are expensive and hard to come by but an imitation lead container can easily be made from an ordinary terracotta or even plastic pot. The technique is primarily paint-based but the addition of real lead embellishments, pressed from a roll of lead, provides a particularly authentic feel. The crucial first step is to choose a container that looks as if it could have been made from lead. If you use terracotta, avoid classic 'terracotta shapes' like the Ali Baba jar or olive jar. If you use plastic, choose a shape with a moulded rim – a thin plastic edge would give the game away.

Making an Imitation Lead Container

Materials

Terracotta or plastic container
Spray can of grey car body cellulose primer
Spray can of chrome car body paint
Small can of oil-based white universal primer
Small can of oil-based matt black paint
Small can of matt polyurethane varnish
White spirit
Small paintbrush, artist's paintbrush
Small roll of gauge 4 lead
Tinsnips
Hard ball and small section of drainpipe or similar to press out decoration
Damp rag
Small bottle of white malt vinegar
All-purpose glue

Preparing the Materials

THINNED GREY PAINT MIX

The grey colour was mixed by adding 10 parts white spirit and 10 parts matt polyurethane varnish to 1 part universal oil-based white primer and 1 part oil-based matt black. In order to achieve the variation of colour characteristic of lead, do not aim for a homogenous blend but instead mix the colours together on the palette as you work so that you achieve a varied streaked effect.

HEAVILY THINNED WHITE PRIMER MIX

Use about 1 part white primer to 15 parts white spirit.

MAKING THE REAL LEAD EMBELLISHMENT

Ideally, wear gloves when handling lead or alternatively wash your hands carefully after use. To make the lead embellishment I placed a circular template on the lead strip and scored around it using a scalpel. Then I cut out the circle of lead using tinsnips. Next I put the lead over the end of a drainpipe and pushed a hard ball that was just larger in diameter than the drainpipe onto the strip of lead to form the rounded indentation, leaving a narrow flat margin around the edge. Finally I weathered the lead to give it a speckled white surface by applying white malt vinegar to the surface using a damp cloth. I applied several coats until the real lead matched the colour of the imitation lead container.

1| *Ensure that the container is dry and then spray the outside all over with grey car body cellulose primer. Spray inside the rim to a depth of no less than 10cm (4in). Leave the container to dry for at least 30 minutes.*

2| *Roughly spray over the first layer of grey primer with the chrome-effect car body paint. Allow to dry for a minimum of 30 minutes.*

Note:
To protect against frost, apply a coat of masonry paint to dry surface before the primer (or bring inside during winter).

6| *When the pot is complete, put a layer of free-draining material at the base and then fill with potting compost to just below the rim. I planted this with Scabiosa 'Butterfly Blue', which looks good against the grey.*

3| *Apply the thinned grey paint mix in vertical strokes, using a small paintbrush, to achieve the streaked 'rain-washed' look typical of weathered lead.*

4| *While the grey is still wet, use the artist's paintbrush, well-loaded with the heavily thinned white primer mix, to flick on white spots to imitate the lead oxide bloom. Then recoat the container with a mixture of matt polyurethane varnish and white primer (1 part paint to 15 parts varnish). Allow to dry for 2 hours.*

5| *Position the real lead embellishment at the centre of one side of the container and secure with all-weather glue. Repeat on the other three sides.*

VERDIGRIS

Verdigris is a finish that occurs naturally when copper or bronze is exposed to the air and a patina of copper acetate forms on the surface, giving a blue-green finish. Because of this it it used to best effect when applied to metal objects. Wood or stone will look most unconvincing when painted with a verdigris finish. Imitating the effect is simply done, and can transform a humble metallic object into a much-prized possession.

There are many different ways to achieve an attractive verdigris finish. The easiest method is simply to apply an emulsion paint such as Fired Earth's Verdigris No. 14, but this alone will not give a very convincing metallic finish. More effective by far is to apply a copper finish and then paint a verdigris-coloured emulsion over it, allowing the metallic copper to come through in places. Also, instead of using a ready-mixed verdigris colour, you could mix viridian green, ultramarine blue and white on a palette as you go along so that you won't get a totally uniform colour. By adding white spirit to thin the paint now and again, you will achieve a highly translucent coat which will allow the copper undercoat to show through where you used lots of white spirit and a more opaque finish where little white spirit was added.

Applying a Verdigris Finish

An old metal bracket suitable for supporting a shelf or a hanging basket was given a face lift and transformed with a simple verdigris finish. The method outlined here is a relatively simple and inexpensive one.

Materials

Wire brush or similar
Copper cellulose spray
Artist's oil paints in viridian green, ultramarine
White oil-based primer
White spirit
Matt clear polyurethane

RIGHT *This chair has been given the verdigris treatment and the green-blue finish is shown off well by the burnt orange background colour of the brickwork. The highlights of orange from the planting add extra zest.*

1| *Brush off the surface to be treated with a wire brush to eliminate flaking paint and other debris. Then sand down with sandpaper or a sandblock and make sure it is clean and dry.*

2| *Spray the surface with a copper cellulose spray and leave to dry. This should take about 15 minutes.*

3| *Make a palette of four parts of viridian green artist's oil paint, one part ultramarine artist's oil paint and one part white oil-based primer. Thin the paint mix with small equal parts of white spirit and matt clear polyurethane to produce a non-uniform paint which is variable in colour and texture.*

4| *The transformed bracket reveals a convincing uneven verdigris colour with subtle copper hints showing through here and there.*

boundaries

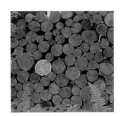 **B**OUNDARIES PROVIDE AN EXCELLENT SPRINGBOARD FOR UTILIZING A WIDE RANGE OF SPECIAL EFFECTS. ALTHOUGH THEIR PRIMARY FUNCTION IS TO DEFINE THE LIMITS OF A GARDEN – OR SECTIONS OF IT – INNOVATIVE DETAILING IN THE USE OF COLOUR, PAINT EFFECTS, TROMPE L'OEIL, MIRRORS AND FINIALS CAN ADD TREMENDOUS PERSONALITY TO A GARDEN. IT IS USE-FUL TO CLARIFY WHAT FUNCTION YOUR BOUNDARY NEEDS TO FULFIL AND USE THIS AS A LEAD FOR THE DETAILING. BOUNDARIES CAN BE MADE TO FULFIL SEVERAL FUNCTIONS AS PLOTS GET SMALLER AND CLOSER TOGETHER. THEY CAN SCREEN EYESORES, PROVIDE BUFFERS AGAINST UNWANTED NOISE AND FILTER DISRUPTIVE WINDS, OR THEY CAN SIMPLY BE 'FUNCTIONAL SCULP-TURES' ADDING A DRAMATIC DIFFERENT DIMENSION TO THE OVERALL PICTURE.

Function & form

A | Solid boundary for screening above eye level

FIG. I Boundary options

C | Tall airy boundary for a small garden in a built-up neighbourhood

B | Solid boundary for screening below eye level

D | Very tall screen to provide privacy at a high level. The lower level screen comes from the hedge behind

RIGHT *An arbour is backed by a stained glass panel in a design by Jon Baillie.*

OPPOSITE LEFT *Ben Wilson's wavy-edged trellis was constructed of old scaffold planks 200mm (8in) wide which were cut with a jigsaw using a rough cut blade. The simple wavy line is sufficient to completely transform the usual rigidity of an off-the-peg trellis panel and contributes to the off-beat informality of the garden.*

OPPOSITE RIGHT (FIG. 2) *Attach the battens to the outside frame using galvanized tacks and when fixing two panels together ensure that the battens butt tightly to form a good join.*

Good fences make good neighbours is only a part of the story. Although fences were traditionally employed to define the limits of a plot of land, their purpose has extended far beyond this original function. Most commonly they are used to afford privacy, in which case a height of 1.8m (6ft) or more will be required. However, designing such a tall screen takes careful thought if it is to be an asset rather than an overbearing eyesore. In tiny plots, a more solid lower section with a see-through upper section helps eliminate the dominance of neighbouring structures without overpowering the garden. In other instances, if the prime object of the fence is to extend the garden visually by connecting it with its surroundings, an invisible boundary (for example a ha-ha) or a very see-through fence will be needed.

Noise may be a problem, and some fences will absorb or deflect some of the sound waves. Planting does not really help, except psychologically, as not being able to see the source of noise distances the noise itself in some way. Earth mounds and solid screens such as walls, on the other hand, considerably lessen the impact of noise. A hedge bank (see page 57) is also ideal – it does not take up too much room and has the added advantage of being relatively inexpensive.

Another important function of boundaries may be to provide shelter. In my hill-top garden, which is regularly subjected to extreme south-westerly gales, the external south-west boundary is designed to filter and slow down the initial impact of the wind, while other internal boundaries on the same orientation back up the filtering effect, creating sheltered spaces which provide favourable growing conditions for more tender plants.

Finally, fences, whether they define boundaries or are simply decorative and used to create smaller spaces within the garden, are ideal for framing views. Often even exceptional views are better defined and emphasized by some walling, piers or planting that draws the eye to where you want to lead it.

SEE-THROUGH BOUNDARIES

A see-through boundary which is not required to screen or provide privacy opens up almost infinite opportunities for original design. The very fact that it is not required to perform a serious practical function encourages a

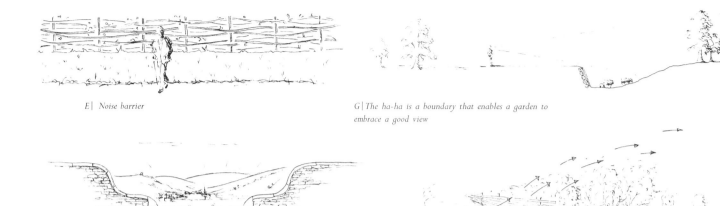

E| Noise barrier

G|The ha-ha is a boundary that enables a garden to embrace a good view

F| A sloping wall can be used to define part of the view while eliminating less appealing elements

H|A boundary can provide a valuable filter for strong winds

more relaxed approach and allows the decorative elements to dominate.

For internal boundaries whose function is primarily to compartmentalize the garden, the wall, hedge or fence can take on quite sculptural characteristics. It might have one or two special sections of stone mixed with more ordinary materials in between and its height can be raised and dropped in order to allow specific views to be framed. Most important of all, an internal boundary, which will not impact on the world outside the garden, can individualize a garden and accentuate its particular style.

In certain environments, even when delineating the boundary of a property, a lighter fence will work well.

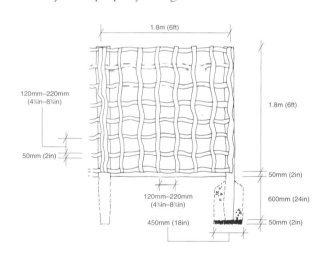

Fig. 2 Ben Wilson's wavy-edged trellis

Trellis battens can be used to form intriguing patterns, especially when you vary the spacing for the gaps slightly, creating a rhythm of generous widths which allow the see-through quality to come into play. Ben Wilson's wavy-edged trellis panelling provides interest and individuality to his own garden while also providing a practical support for twining plants and for tying in climbers.

ABOVE *A typical example of a highly detailed brick wall with buttresses and an archway at The Old Vicarage, East Ruston. Note the sloping brick coping, and the smaller buttresses appearing to give emphasis to the arch.*

RIGHT *The Postman's Entrance at the Old Vicarage, East Ruston. All the archways are different and this one is the most splendid, utilizing this grand crest, tile coping, finials, brick crenellations and a very strong design element.*

Designer Tips

Curved Brickwork
If the radius of the brick curve is smaller than about 1.3m (4ft 3in) headers should be used (normal 215mm [9in] bricks used head on) to achieve the curve, otherwise the brick ends will project slightly from the wall (which is not unattractive). Alternatively, special radial bricks can be used. They give a more precise appearance but are more expensive. Radial bricks are commonly available to fit outer edge radii from 45cm (18in) to 540cm (17ft 7in). Radial bricks for smaller radii can be made to order.

RIGHT *The half round reconstituted stone finial is given extra emphasis by the use of projecting brickwork beneath the tile coping. The wall has two courses of projecting tiles under a simple tile on edge coping. Brick can be an expensive material and deserves careful thought for the detailing to really work.*

have to be formed from a brick or stone wall. I used reclaimed telegraph poles for ours (see page 53). At the Menagerie, they simply dug out a V-shaped trench to a depth of approximately 1.2m (4ft) and sunk a post and wire fence in the bottom to keep livestock out, hiding it from view totally unless you get very near the edge.

BARRIER BOUNDARIES

Solid barriers are effective for blocking out unsightly views, reducing noise and wind, and affording privacy. A walled garden generates a feeling of enclosure and cloistered protection which is achieved by obliterating all unwanted external factors and focusing the attention on the internal detail within.

Walls

The physical density and durability of stone and brick makes these materials an obvious choice when creating a solid barrier. There are numerous ways of ringing the changes with walls of this sort, ensuring that they have a distinct character as well as performing an important function. As well as subtle variations in the types of coursing used (see Figs 4 and 5, pages 55 and 56) you can also create great impact by thoughtful attention to details such as coping, ornamentation, inscription or by adding major features like piers, buttresses, archways and peepholes.

If you have sufficient room to make it work, a serpentine wall adds a dynamic feel to the garden. As well as providing visual interest in its own right, a curved wall creates sheltered niches for a wide range of tender plants that will perform well, protected from the wind and enjoying the warmth generated by heat-retentive stones or bricks. An alternative alignment for interest might be to step the wall in and out at right angles.

To make a boundary wall really special, employ a letter carver (see Suppliers' Guide) to etch a few appropriate words. The size of the lettering needs to be quite bold so that it stands out. Quotations, Latin mottos, special dates or words commemorating a particular event are popular choices.

STONEWORK

Building stone walls is a skilled job which rewards careful attention to the detailing from the start. Build, or ask your stonemason to build, a small sample panel first, and let the mortar dry to check the colour. As a general

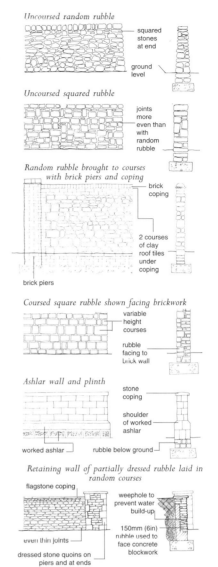

Uncoursed random rubble

squared
stones
at end

ground
level

Uncoursed squared rubble

joints
more
even than
with
random
rubble

Random rubble brought to courses
with brick piers and coping

brick
coping

2 courses
of clay
roof tiles
under
coping

brick piers

Coursed square rubble shown facing brickwork

variable
height
courses

rubble
facing to
brick wall

Ashlar wall and plinth

stone
coping

shoulder
of worked
ashlar

worked ashlar — rubble below ground

Retaining wall of partially dressed rubble laid in
random courses

flagstone coping

weephole to
prevent water
build-up

150mm (6in)
rubble used to
face concrete
blockwork

even thin joints

dressed stone quoins on
piers and at ends

FIG. 4 *Stone wall coursing options*

LEFT *'The Wall That Went for a Walk', designed by Andy Goldsworthy for Grizedale Sculpture Park, Cumbria.*

BELOW *An entrance formed from dressed stone quoins cut to form a simple roll moulding around the arch. Beautifully laid coursed random rubble stonework forms the rest of the wall, with the mortar well recessed.*

BOTTOM *This panel of wisdom inserted in a beautiful piece of rubble walling is in Ian Hamilton Finlay's garden, Little Sparta, near Edinburgh.*

rule, try to re-create the type of stonework that is on the main house, especially if the wall is close to it, or else copy the form of stone walling that is indigenous to the area.

Subtle variations in the overall effect of a wall can be achieved through the style of coursing, from informal uncoursed random rubble through to the even geometric look of ashlar (see Fig. 4). Ashlar is a very expensive type of walling. The stone is cut to exact sizes, with smooth, flat faces, so the joints are minimal. It is most commonly used in urban environments or for important buildings.

Types of stonework

Figure 4 illustrates different types of stonework, the first being uncoursed random rubble with squared stones at the returned ends. Uncoursed squared rubble tends to have joints of more even thickness. Random rubble brought to courses and used with brick piers and coping is an attractive method. Coursed squared rubble is used to describe a wall in which the courses vary in height. An ashlar wall is enhanced with a plinth of worked stone and a stone coping. Finally a concrete block retaining wall is faced with coursed rubble and finished with stone quoins on the piers — as stone is fairly expensive this is a wise way to reduce costs.

Rubble is the term used for stone which is uncut, or has been cut very roughly, so that the individual stones are all different shapes and sizes. Dry stone walls are an example of rubble walling. In rubble walls where mortar is used the joints will all be different sizes, so it is better if the mortar is recessed and its colour blends in with the stones, so it is as inconspicuous as possible. This can be achieved by choosing a suitably coloured sand or using coloured cement. It takes a very long time to lay rubble in courses, but the finished effect is well worth the effort. The stone can be partially dressed, in which case a stonemason will have shaped each stone with a hammer, enabling a wall to be built with very narrow, tight joints. Piers with quoins or corner stones made of dressed stone, two or three times the size of the rest of the stones of the wall, can be added for style.

BRICKWORK

A brick wall, rather than a stone one, may be more in keeping with your house. If you opt for a brick wall, remember that a large part of the character of a wall will depend on the type of brick used, though elaborate copings and types of coursework can also affect the overall look and style. Bricks can be hand-made and rustic or regular and precise. Most manufacturers have a range of specially shaped bricks and, for a price, will make up virtually anything you want.

A skilled bricklayer will know how to lay strapwork (project bricks in a wall so as to form letters, circles or squares) and introduce other interesting variations to break up the monotony of a large length of wall. However, there are also easier ways in which to stamp an individual mark on your boundary walls: murals can be made with specially made bricks, or by cutting bricks; different-coloured bricks can be incorporated at random or regular distances; and decorative, embossed bricks can be included.

Hedges

Tall, solid hedges are cheaper than walls and can be just as effective as solid boundaries. Again, departing from a normal straight line will immediately make your boundary more interesting. Topiary (see page 106) will create a sense of drama and will also work well with the living green 'walls'. Combining stone with hedging will produce a wonderful blend of the hard and the soft. Using hedging as the main boundary and flanking it with stone piers, as has been done at Les Jardins du Manoir d'Eryignac, near Sarlat in

France, visually strengthens the whole structure and gives it gravitas.

In my garden, I built chunky stone piers, linked them with a timber beam, and infilled the gap with yew hedging. The piers defined the boundary instantly, and the planting will add its weight in the fullness of time. At Groombridge Place in Kent, niches have been carved into the hedge and busts placed in them (see opposite). This has added a solid element as well as a foil to the green.

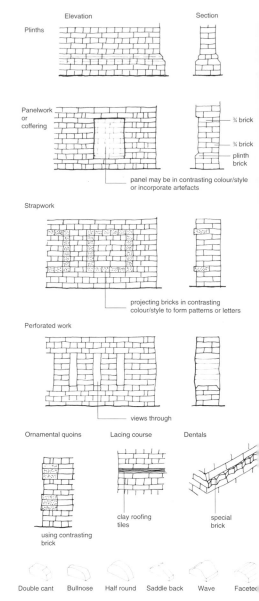

FIG. 5 *Brickwork courses*

RIGHT (FIG. 5) There is plenty of scope for adding interest to brickwork. Starting from the top: plinths have the effect of making a wall look much more substantial and also give added strength; panelwork stops a wall looking monotonous and is ideal for displaying artefacts; strapwork involves slightly projecting bricks usually of a different colour — they can be arranged to form patterns and letters; perforated work allows views to be glimpsed through and lightens the appearance of a wall; ornamental quoins give the wall a solid feel; copings are available in many different shapes and sizes to finish the top of a wall.

BELOW These generously sized brick piers are given added interest by using regularly projecting courses of brickwork. The finials too are given greater weight by using four courses of cantilevered tiles in ever-increasing sizes.

Hedge Banks

Hedge banks, which combine a solid bank with living plants, make excellent sound barriers, provided the banks are deep enough. One successful combination is to form the bank from two woven panels lined with marine ply. Pack this with earth and plant hedging on top. The soil within the panels must be well compacted in successive layers, otherwise settlement will make it fall away from the plant roots. Expert assistance with the construction is available (see Suppliers' Guide). Regular irrigation will be necessary to keep the hedge healthy.

Willow hedge banks look most attractive, particularly soon after planting. They need a deep bank 60–90cm (2–3ft) deep, angled at no more than 70°, and broad on top to prevent drying out. Provided they are well-tended, regularly watered and cut back in early spring, they are visually pleasing and an effective sound barrier, at least in the short term. However, plants inevitably die out over the years, leaving a residual core of a few stronger specimens, causing many people to become disenchanted with willow hedging. Alternatively, you can weave a hedge bank with cut willow.

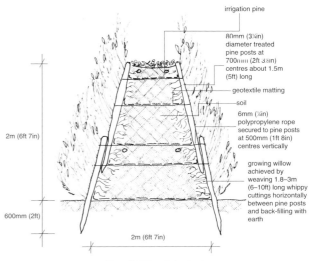

irrigation pine

80mm (3¼in) diameter treated pine posts at 700mm (2ft 3¼in) centres about 1.5m (5ft) long

geotextile matting

soil

6mm (¼in) polypropylene rope secured to pine posts at 500mm (1ft 8in) centres vertically

growing willow achieved by weaving 1.8–3m (6–10ft) long whippy cuttings horizontally between pine posts and back-filling with earth

2m (6ft 7in)

600mm (2ft)

2m (6ft 7in)

FIG. 6 *Willow hedge bank*

Deception with boundaries

MAKING STONE GO FURTHER

Local stone is an ideal building material in a stone area. It has a magical quality in garden situations, maybe because of its solid, permanent nature, which contrasts strongly with soft areas of planting. It is incredibly flexible, as Gothic religious buildings prove, but it is very costly. A little good detailing in stone, however, goes a long way in a garden context. Site it prominently and use less expensive, unobtrusive finishes in conjunction with it; use planting to hide the latter and emphasize the former.

As an alternative to the real thing, reconstructed cast concrete stone is often used. Personally I don't favour this option. If my budget is limited, I prefer to use rendered concrete blocks and finish them with a few courses of real stone and a stone coping, ideally even incorporating stone piers or stone buttresses.

Another way to achieve the appearance of stone boundaries on a reduced budget is painted stone blocking (see page 31). This is an excellent way to fake stonework on a rendered surface, and works well for external boundary walls where plants can help blur the difference between the fake and the real.

AN ILLUSION OF SPACE

In confined areas, where 'real' space is limited, there are various ways in which one can create an illusion of space. One option is to make parallel side boundaries converge at a gentle angle as they move away from the most common viewpoint, usually the house. The obvious drawback is that this trick also works in reverse: when viewed from the bottom of the garden, the angled boundaries will have a shortening effect.

Adding a gate or a door to a boundary where no access exists gives the impression that there is somewhere further to go. Take this idea one stage further by including mirrors in the doorway: their reflection will create enticing glimpses of the 'next' garden. Trompe l'oeil, either surrounded by a trellis or painted onto a flat surface, is an effective and intriguing way to push out flat boundaries and create an illusory sense of depth.

RIGHT *This is one of my favourite details. The organic architecture of the curved hedge is finished off with these small stone pillars – an inexpensive boundary but an extremely effective one.*

RIGHT *A rendered concrete block wall is less expensive than stone, but here the stone coping and small areas of stone on the wall ends contribute greatly to the overall appearance of the wall without increasing the cost too dramatically. The pale yellow flowers of the* Cytisus battandieri *look good against the Tuscan pink background.*

Detailing

In many instances it is details which set an item apart from the ordinary and make it stand out. We have seen how originality can be applied to walls through coursing options, getting the coping right and paying special attention to details like the colour of the mortar. Once the established framework of your boundary is in place, it is time to consider gates, peepholes, hinges, posts and finials.

GATES AND DOORS

Successful gardens are often composed of a combination of different spaces which give you a feeling of excited anticipation as you wander from one to the other. Gates help to define these areas. Sometimes they allow you an alluring glimpse through or over them. If they are totally solid they encourage you to open them to discover what is beyond. A solid door with a smallish peephole invites you to look and makes the design of the door more interesting without greatly reducing security or privacy. Peepholes can be any shape – diamond, oval, triangular – and can be open, glazed, or filled with trellis.

FAR RIGHT *Wonderfully elaborate metal hinges are the icing on the cake for this enticing doorway. Graham Robeson and Alan Gray at the Old Vicarage, East Ruston, have finished the metal with their own particular blue/grey paint to give it their hallmark.*

RIGHT *This hefty lump of stone with a naturally occurring ammonite in it was a fortuitous find for Marnie Hall and her team when they were creating their 'Quarryman's garden' for the Chelsea Flower Show 1998.*

BELOW *This chunky old wooden gatepost adds charm to a simple rustic gate, showing how a small amount of detail can go a long way.*

If you can accommodate several gates in your garden, link them visually by making them similar in some respects but different in others. At the Old Vicarage in East Ruston, for example, most of the gates are made from solid oak, with feature hinges of different designs, but all are painted the same stunning blue. Another way to add an original touch to timber gates is to incorporate metal bars in them. This makes them look lighter and less rustic.

There are other ways to improve gates. A new coat of paint in a more interesting colour can completely transform the impression a gate makes, while an entirely new character can be created by adding huge and/or ornamental metal hinges, and perhaps an intricate handle. Many blacksmiths are a good source of modern and traditional designs for ironmongery and can give you guidance in this area (see Suppliers' Guide).

  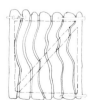

FIG. 7 *Gate designs. (The 'wavy' design can be seen on page 34.)*

Boundary Posts

The upright posts are an important part of any fence, gateway or boundary line. In fact, if you get these right you can often get away with less-than-perfect fence panels because it is the uprights that dominate.

Gateposts can be made to look so strong that they can stand on their own, obviating the need for a gate in some situations. To make this work in timber, they need to be heavy (around 150 × 150mm [6 × 6in]) and would benefit from a slightly larger than usual capping with a bold carved finial. Brick and stone pillars look weightier if they are boldly detailed.

There are other ways to make the upright posts dominate: by making the fence panels lower and simpler; by painting colour on the posts, but not on the fence; and by ornamentation such as bun-turned or chamfered edges.

ABOVE *This gate made from garden tools adds a decorative touch of humour to the garden. It was designed by George Carter.*

ABOVE RIGHT *These gates at Clipsham House form an eye-catching entrance to a meadow. The two gentle curves of the fence and the gate lead up to emphasize the finials. The curved metal hinges are picked out in black, ensuring that they stand out.*

RIGHT *A solid gateway with bold crenellations gives a barbican-like feel to this entrance. It contrasts strongly with the light, enticing gate which encourages you to glimpse through and enjoy the view beyond.*

ABOVE *The huge Gothic timber finials on this building at The Menagerie, at Horton in Northamptonshire, break up the large dome of thatch and greatly embellish the building. Note the effective stone blocking on the rendered wall behind the pillars.*

BELOW *These mass-produced timber birds have been individualized to fit in with the colour theme. The heavy ropes which link the posts are available from a rope specialist, Footrope Knots (see Suppliers' Guide).*

FIG. 8 *Decorative finials*

Tall metal spike

Metal pineapple

Metal spear

Two-dimensional star in timber or metal

Terracotta or stone finial with collared base

Two-dimensional timber cherubs painted to appear three-dimensional

Timber finial

Pyramids in terracotta, stone or wood

Terracotta or stone pineapple

Decorative stone finial

Stone bud

Split stone ball

Timber pyramid with small ball

Metal boar

Metal 'spade' shape

Decorative metal ball with spike

FINIALS

Prominently sited on top of gateposts, walls and other high structures, finials make a considerable impact, so thoughtful selection is essential. Finials were popular with the Greeks and the Romans, who used many figurative shapes, often involving acanthus leaves and scrolls. During the High Gothic period, many finials and pinnacles were lavishly detailed, both in stone and wood. In Victorian England quite modest homes and gardens were decorated with carved wood, terracotta or stone finials, often of geometric shapes. Traditional finials can be used today to evoke a timeless permanence, while modern unique motifs can generate a sense of theatre.

Stone finials in particular have a sense of permanence about them. They are often seen on churches and other historic buildings, emphasizing the apex of a roof, pediment or gable and showing the effects of exposure to the elements for centuries. Stone finials can also be of modern or abstract design, although because of the high

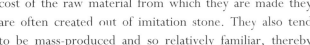

cost of the raw material from which they are made they are often created out of imitation stone. They also tend to be mass-produced and so relatively familiar, thereby losing some impact.

Timber, being less expensive and easier to carve than stone, is a popular material for finials. It is less likely to be used for huge one-off ornamental features, but is favoured in a repeating context, perhaps along a line of fencing. Hardwood finials will last for many years, especially if they are not subjected to constant damp. Tannelized softwood finials are cheaper and easier to carve, but will not last as long.

Terracotta is inexpensive and ideal for finial shapes such as pineapples, obelisks, pyramids and balls. These are available off the peg in various sizes, or from Whichford Pottery which will make any terracotta finial to order (see Suppliers' Guide). In particular some Italian catalogues produce a huge range of items. If orange is not in your colour scheme, or you want to disguise the fact that they are terracotta, you can paint them with masonry paint or tinted limewash (see page 28).

Wrought iron and cast iron are frequently made into extravagant yet visually light ornamental finials, often picked out in a colour such as gold or verdigris to give them extra weight. They are commonly used on metal objects such as railings, aviaries or plant supports, but occasionally they can be seen on the apex of tiled roofs. Lead and bronze are traditionally used for finials, combining well aesthetically with most structural materials. They are also ideal in modern gardens.

Fake Finishes

The late David Hicks designed and made his own fake stone finials from marine ply, finished in a stone-coloured matt gloss. As they are usually placed high up and are beautifully proportioned, they look very convincingly like stone.

Finials made from moulded plastic can be passed off as metal if they are given a black paint finish. Glass spheres with lighting inside are functional as well as attractive. Decorative plant pots can have ivies trained around a spherical metal framework in a tub; balls made from two hanging baskets fitted back-to-back can be filled with compost and planted with low-growing thyme; sea urchin shells can be filled with plaster and fixed on wooden posts – the possibilities are infinite.

ARCHES

Arches, whether traditional or modern, rustic or grand, are a superb element to include in a garden. They can frame views or link spaces. They also give you tremendous scope to add an intrinsically pleasing element to highlight entrances and walkways. There is no need to be conventional in your detailing of them. They add another dimension to modern or traditional schemes, and they also provide plenty of scope for bringing in a theatrical element to adorn your garden if that is what you desire. There are many different types of arches, and the drawings in Fig. 9 (page 65) illustrate 10 of them. If you wish to explore the subject of arches further, you can do no better than to refer to Sir Banister Fletcher's *A History of Architecture* for at least 35 different types.

When you are deciding upon a style of archway, you first need to establish what overall effect you are wanting to achieve. If you are aiming at an appearance of tradition and formality, you should take your cue from the shape and materials of any arches which already exist in the house. At Stapleford Park in Leicestershire, where the entrances through the high brick of the walled garden were three-centred arches, I designed metal structures of the same shape and size and positioned several of them over the two main paths to link the four main entrances.

RIGHT *These half balls are made from reconstructed stone which has a pink tinge. Some manufacturers, such as Grosvenor Stone (see Suppliers' Guide), will colour their reconstructed stone to match a stone sample, which creates a far more authentic look from day one.*

BELOW *In a Chelsea Flower Show garden, the tropical theme was carried through using sea urchin shells as finials. If I were to use them in a real garden I would fill them with mastic to give them substance and help protect them. A huge range of shells is available from the Shell Factory (see Suppliers' Guide).*

surfaces

 **H**ARD SURFACES IN A GARDEN PLAY A VERY IMPORTANT PRACTICAL FUNCTION: THEY FACILITATE ACCESS. HOWEVER THE AREA THAT THEY TAKE UP IN A GARDEN IS QUITE SUBSTANTIAL, AND THEIR DESIGN HAS A MAJOR IMPACT ON THE CHARACTER OF A SPACE. PEOPLE OFTEN CONCENTRATE ON THE FUNCTIONAL ASPECT ONLY, AND FORGET THAT HERE IS A GOLDEN OPPORTUNITY TO SELECT FROM THE VAST RANGE OF EXCITING MATERIALS AND ADD YEAR-ROUND STYLE AND DISTINCTION TO A GARDEN. YOU WILL PROBABLY SEE AND USE YOUR SURFACES EVERY DAY, ESPECIALLY THOSE NEAR THE HOUSE, SO MAKE SURE YOU GO FOR GOLD AT THE OUTSET. SURFACES FORM THE BARE BONES OF THE GARDEN, AND WORK BEST IF THEY ARE GENEROUSLY PROPORTIONED AND BEAUTIFULLY DETAILED. WHEN THOUGHTFULLY SELECTED THEY CAN ENDURE A LIFETIME.

Traditional materials

GRAVEL

Gravel is one of the most commonly used materials for hard surfaces. It is relatively inexpensive, and its soft, informal appearance is incredibly adaptable, suiting tiny rustic cottages through to grand estates. There are many ways in which it can be dressed up for unusual effect.

Raked Gravel

Gravel raked in a pattern gives a very formal appearance. I know a French château with an immaculate courtyard made of grey and white gravel, raked meticulously in alternating lines. It looks superb, but unless you find the exercise spiritually therapeutic, the constant raking is hugely time-consuming. Perhaps it is best to create patterns only in areas which are not walked on very often, such as a visible but fairly inaccessible roof terrace. The pattern can then be highlighted with the addition of other pebbles, boulders, or different-coloured gravel.

Bound Gravel

Many people love the informal nature of loose gravel, but are put off by its downsides: it kicks around, sticks to shoes and gets into the house, wrecks high heels and needs frequent, regular raking if it is to look its best. To avoid these disadvantages, you could try using bound gravel; it is slightly more expensive, but is in many ways more practical.

RIGHT *Breedon gravel is a bound gravel that is even suitable for wheelchairs, as demonstrated here in The Bird Garden for the elderly which I designed for the Chelsea Flower Show 1997, where I used it edged with stone. It is available from Breedon plc (see Suppliers' Guide).*

Method 1: Breedon Gravel

One way to bind gravel is to select a gravel or hoggin that has 15mm (⅝in) angular particles grading down to dust. (I often use golden-buff Breedon – see Suppliers' Guide). Lay it by rolling it while running water floods the surface, so it sets hard when it dries. It makes an attractive surface, particularly if edged or patterned with bricks, slabs or setts. If it is in a shady situation you might need to use moss killer occasionally.

Method 2: Colas System

An alternative option is to lay a well-compacted base of 15–40mm (⅝–1½in) clean angular stone, spray it with cold bituminous emulsion (black liquid tar), and then cover it with 9–12mm (⅜–½in) granite or other hard chippings which are immediately rolled in. Next day the surface is rolled again and swept and sprayed with another coat of bituminous emulsion which is then immediately covered with clean washed 6–9mm (¼–⅜in) shingle and rolled well again. If there is a lot of traffic the surface will tend to come loose in places, but it can always be redone as necessary, every other year or so. I have used this method to cover existing areas of tarmac and concrete as a cheap alternative to lifting them. It is a good system, but there tend to be a few loose particles left kicking about.

Method 3: Resin-bonded gravel

With this approach you incorporate a resin and suitably coloured or clear hardener with a 7mm (¼in) layer of small-size gravel and lay it on top of a concrete or dense tarmacadam surface, leaving it to set. You can do this yourself or use a specialist firm (see Suppliers' Guide). The surface is suitable for vehicular and pedestrian use, and costs about the same as reproduction stone slabs.

Patterns with Gravels

Decorative aggregates come in a variety of colours: dark grey-green, sparkling white, rusty red, brown, grey, yellow and gold. They also come in a variety of sizes and shapes. They can be used to create strong-coloured patterns with paving or low hedging to separate each section. If you use paving, make the finished gravel level 5mm (⅜in) lower so the different colours don't slip across and mix, or roll the chippings into colas as for bound gravel (Method 2 above). Alternatively, make these patterns where there is not much traffic.

Plants in Gravel

Gravel shows off certain plants to their best advantage, especially plants that are at home in a free-draining environment. An informal effect can be achieved by spreading a larger gravel (including a few pebbles or boulders if a beachy feel is wanted) around drifts of plants, thus protecting them by demarcating their space, and then using a smaller gravel for the path. Geometric or informal shapes can be formed in this way, and dwarf hedges of lavender, box or germander interspersed with clipped topiary are ideal plant choices.

ABOVE *This is a form of bound gravel where the gravel is fixed down with a bituminous emulsion. I incorporated a pattern of York flags into the design of the drive to transform it more into a courtyard than a turning circle.*

TOP RIGHT *This paving has a strong rhythm, with timber breaking up the expanse of pale grey chippings. It also provides a good area for colonization by these grasses. The design is by Christopher Bradley-Hole.*

RIGHT *Here is a clever use of exposed aggregate concrete. The concrete panels were formed in irregular blocks and then laid with a mix of gravel and pebbles, making it a very economic path. A few pebbles are fun to include and, as can be seen, go a long way.*

FAR RIGHT *In Sir Roy Strong's garden a bold livery of blue and yellow is used, which he has continued through to the coloured glass chippings he has used to edge this parterre. Glass chippings provide a good range of colours (see Suppliers' Guide).*

CONCRETE

Concrete has had a bad press in gardening circles, especially when used as a paving material. It is often laid extensively but unimaginatively, and the resulting dull expanse of solid grey with shabby edges does it no favours. In fact, when used in small quantities with a contrasting material and attractively finished, it can be more than acceptable.

Exposed Aggregate Finish

Concrete particularly benefits from the addition of a strongly textured material. For example, add gravels, granites, limestones, slates or pea shingle to the concrete. The appearance will vary dramatically according to the material used. The proportions should be 1:2:4 cement to sand to aggregate. If you expose the aggregate by wire brushing it as the concrete begins to stiffen and then using a hose as the concrete becomes harder, the added aggregate becomes the most dominant material on the surface. A weak solution of hydrochloric acid, which you can buy already diluted as brick or patio cleaner from any brick merchant, will clear any milky appearance between the aggregate. I have seen exposed aggregate concrete effectively used in randomly sized rectangles to form a path of irregular width, broken with parallel bands of pebbles set in mortar; it was most attractive.

Coloured Concrete

The colour of the concrete depends on the aggregate, sand and cement used. If a nondescript material is employed the concrete will be grey. However, you can colour the grey from a range of over 40 different pigments available from builders' merchants (do not exceed the amount of pigment recommended in the manufacturers' instructions or the overall effect will be very brash). As with exposed aggregate, coloured concrete works best when mixed with other materials. For example, alternate wide bands of concrete with railway sleepers, setts, bricks, shells or crushed glass to form a simple repetitive pattern.

MIXING MATERIALS

Paving slabs and brick are the most popular materials for hard areas, but unfortunately they are often laid in a very mundane way, especially reproduction slabs. However, an exceptionally good reproduction slab (see

ABOVE Here concrete has been used to great effect – the circular stepping stones have been surrounded by circles made from a small paving unit. With the gravel surround, it forms an unusual, practical and economical path.

ABOVE RIGHT Grass mixes with paving extremely well. Here the green sward flows into the hard paving and creates a simple but eye-catching pattern. Make sure the soil is about 5–10mm (¼–½in) proud of the paving so the mower can run over the slabs, negating the need for laborious edging up.

BELOW RIGHT This bold design by Hiroshi Nanamori and Andrew Butcher shows how effective gravel can be when mixed with other materials. Interlocking rectangular granite blocks are softened by the surrounding gravel. The bold shapes of clipped box enhance the strong design.

Suppliers' Guide) can be combined with small quantities of more unusual materials to create an effective, even dramatic, paved area at an affordable price.

Always avoid using reproduction materials on their own because they are too conspicuous. Mix them with other materials in a strong pattern, so as to distract the eye: diamonds, squares, rectangles or strong repeating bands all work well. Brick, granite setts, stone setts and coloured glass chippings are ideal partners to slabs. You could also try close-carpeting plants such as *Thymus minimus*, *Sagina glabra* or *Chamaemelum nobile* 'Treneague', used in bold block bands and patterns, exactly as you would a hard material.

BRICK

Brick paving gives an attractive, hard-wearing, non-slip surface. It can be laid flat or on edge, in several variations of basketweave, herringbone, stack bond, running bond or other designs. Patterns can be emphasized further by using different-coloured bricks.

For something more unusual you can inset bricks with patterns on them, such as a leaf or a rose. These are readily available (see Suppliers' Guide) and can be used for the whole path, but work better if they are used only at the margins or in distinct areas.

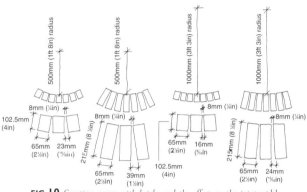

FIG 10 *Creating curves with bricks and the effect on the joint width*

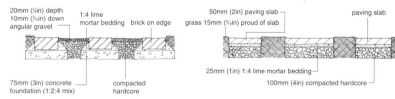

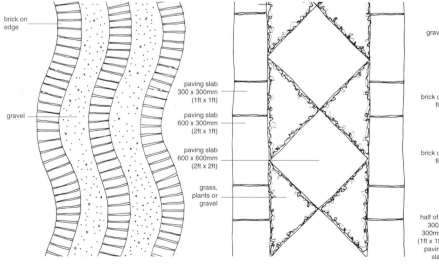

FIG 11 *Paving options for paths*

TIMBER DECKING

Timber decking gives a wonderfully, clean, modern look to a garden. In wetter climates, a common concern is the slippery nature of wood. In reality, wood is no more slippery than York stone, and decking has regular gaps which help your foot to grip. These gaps also resolve drainage problems. While I would not recommend decking for an old people's home, it should not be a problem for normal domestic use.

The expansive feel that an area of decking creates is due to the total flatness of the surface and its beautifully clean, straight lines. Left to weather naturally, it becomes a soft silver-grey which works well with the organic yellows, reds and browns of most buildings.

SITUATION

A deck can be virtually any shape or size, which means it can be accommodated into awkward areas. It is also possible to incorporate existing features such as trees into the design of a deck. You can have a sweeping curve, a zigzag or a serpentine line. Alternatively, you can choose to reflect certain shapes of the house, or perhaps a swimming pool, for example.

Decking is the perfect surface for roof terraces for practical as well as aesthetic reasons. In situations where there is no existing perimeter fencing, you can attach new fencing fixtures to the horizontal decking joists, in effect cantilevering them in position. This eliminates the need to attach a fence to the building structure itself, which can cause problems.

If you put in a deck at first-floor level, make sure the space underneath it does not become redundant but has a function of its own too.

Choice of Timber

The choice of timber is important. Western red cedar will not need preservative pressure impregnation, and will quickly weather to an attractive silvery grey before slowly becoming darker over the years. Scandinavian redwoods need preservative treatment and tend to weather in a less attractive, rather dirty-looking fashion. Reclaimed American pitch pine is supposed to be totally non-slip and weathers very attractively, but is expensive.

Detailing

Although decking photographs well, it is often difficult to carry it off in reality. It is important to maintain the feeling of lightness and elevation which you get, particularly from a raised deck. When considering balustrades and other ways to define the edge of the deck, choose pale-coloured woods or finishes and subtle styles. These will link with the sky, or the rest of the garden at ground level, and maintain the clean-lined spacious feel. If you are 'fencing' the deck, use thin-section vertical and horizontal timbers as widely centred as you can afford so that the area feels part of what is beyond.

Patterns and Paint Effects

Decking can be painted, but it looks tired and worn quite quickly and requires regular maintenance. If you want to colour it, use a translucent woodstain, and restrict the application to those areas which are less used. A better way to break up uniformity is to make patterns with the wood itself, laying the timber in different widths, at oblique angles, in squares or rectangles.

Other Timber Paving

Log rounds set vertically in the ground create a strong rustic feel. They should be made of a durable hardwood, a good 15cm (6in) deep and a minimum diameter of 45cm (18in). They will last longer if you remove the bark. Patterns can be picked out by grading them into sizes and using the groups in courses, as in stonework (see page 55). The gaps between them can be filled with sand, gravel or shells. Small, size-sorted pebbles could be fitted into the gaps in simple patterns. The gaps can be filled in with plants such as *Soleirolia soleirolii*. This will look very good, but the humidity of the soil will make the logs rot relatively quickly. Shells, sand and gravel with their free-draining characteristics will ensure a longer life. Logs do become slippery and they are not the easiest of surfaces to walk on in smart shoes, but their charm depends on their irregular, organic feel, which is particularly suitable in more rustic areas.

In an Oxford garden I saw railway sleepers alternating with gravel, arranged as paving around the base of a huge specimen tree in a radiating pattern. They provided an excellent finish to what would otherwise have been a difficult area.

OPPOSITE This low-key decking works well as a functional and attractive edge to the water. It is broken in places by bands of aggregate to reinforce the strong linear pattern. It was designed by David Stevens.

ABOVE This decking area looks more dramatic in real life, perched up above a wide river, providing an exhilarating spot for meals. The timber used for the decking is keruing, a moderately dense hardwood, while the structure has been built from tannelized softwood. It was built by Mike Harvey (see Suppliers' Guide) for Murray Leach's dramatic Cotswold garden.

FAR RIGHT A paved timber path forms a gentle curve. The gaps between a small width of timber ensure that it is a lot less slippery than wide timber tightly jointed. This works even when no gravel is used.

ORGANIC MATERIALS

Organic materials are ideal for making a natural, understated impression. Ammonite shapes made from high quality terracotta (see Suppliers' Guide) are interesting and suitable for use in modest quantities or small areas. They come mixed in a range of different sizes, from 300 to 40mm (12 to 1½in), and are about 70mm (2¾in) thick. Interlock the various sizes as you lay them on a mortar bed, keeping the joints as small as possible. They can be set in spiral patterns or interspersed in gravel or other types of hard paving.

Pebbles are wonderful to use for paving, but require careful handling. A large expanse of pebble paving can be hard to walk on, but if you thread lines of pebbles through other materials, a brilliant effect is achieved (see below right). Pebbles are fairly expensive to buy, and commercial suppliers do not always stock the exact shapes and sizes required. Seek permission before removing pebbles from a beach.

By mixing them with other materials your hard-won pebbles will go further. Hard-wearing stones such as limestone, granite, flint or quartz are good companions – the flat planes of the stones make a satisfying contrast with the rounded pebbles. Avoid soft, grainy sandstones and shales. Tiles placed on end, such as riven slate, are suitable, and so are stoneware tiles cut in strips and ceramic shards, with their linear flat finish. All of these materials can be effectively woven into a pebble design. Gravels from builders' merchants that are eroded and worn by water mix extremely well with pebbles. They are useful to fill awkward or tiny spaces, or they can surround areas of pebbles pressed into wet concrete.

Shells are great fun to use and can be bought by the kilogram, sack or lorry-load (see Suppliers' Guide). A wide variety is available as a by-product of food

FAR RIGHT TOP *In my courtyard garden I included this small area of ammonites which are made from high-quality terracotta as used by makers in 18th-century England and bedded on a dry sand/cement mix. (See Suppliers' Guide.) I used small (at most 5mm/¼in) angular, golden gravel to fill in the gaps.*

FAR RIGHT CENTRE *This small area of tile paving on edge is made from offcuts from Collyweston stone roof tiles, which come from Collyweston in Lincolnshire. The joints are formed from recessed mortar and I included an old flowerpot rim in the centre. The tile offcuts are now available from David Ellis (see Suppliers' Guide).*

FAR RIGHT BELOW *This informal arrangement of loose pebbles, randomly shaped stone paving and plants creates an interesting organic area of paving.*

RIGHT *This narrow path runs through my children's garden close to their sand-pit and so a cockleshell surface seemed like a good idea. They are laid about 25mm (1in) deep on about 75mm (3in) of hardcore. They crush down with wear so after a few months you have crushed shells on the well-trodden areas and large shells on the edge. They do not harm mower blades. See Suppliers' Guide.*

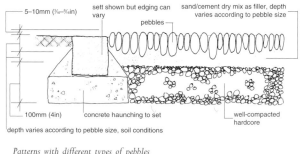

FIG 12 *Laying a pebble surface*

5–10mm (¾₆–⅜in) | sett shown but edging can vary | sand/cement dry mix as filler, depth varies according to pebble size

pebbles

100mm (4in) | concrete haunching to set depth varies according to pebble size, soil conditions | well-compacted hardcore

Patterns with different types of pebbles

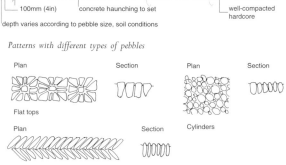

Plan | Section | Plan | Section

Flat tops

Plan | Section | Cylinders

Stimmers or longs

RIGHT *This path of concrete slabs, with a small, repeating inset pattern of pale and dark blue, is in Ian Hamilton Finlay's innovative garden.*

FAR RIGHT ABOVE *This area of paving incorporates slabs, bricks and blue tiles. The latter tie in with the blue colour scheme which prevails elsewhere in the garden. It was designed by Keeyla Meadows.*

FAR RIGHT BELOW *Pebble paving laid in this extravagant fashion contributes tremendously to the mood of the space. Great care has been spent on detailing.*

processing. Cockleshells, which are relatively inexpensive, form an interesting surface for a path. They are soft, so if they stray onto the lawn they won't damage mower blades. They do crush down with use and become unrecognizable, but even then they still look quite pleasant. Shells work well with log rounds where they fill the awkward, variable-shaped gaps left by juxtaposing the logs together. When selecting materials for this purpose I use mixed shells, as they retain their shape well.

MOSAICS

Small areas of elaborately ornamental mosaics can be worked into other forms of paving, perhaps to edge a path, or to form a small central panel to bring a burst of colour to your surfaces. Mosaic pieces can be made of any hard, non-porous material, such as bits of reject or broken tiles, ceramics fired to stoneware temperatures, glass marbles, pebbles or stones.

Although making mosaics for the garden is not difficult, if you would rather commission an expert, the National Register of Makers from the Crafts Council (see Suppliers' Guide) will be able to recommend someone in your area. This option tends to be fairly expensive, but a small, special piece of mosaic set amongst more ordinary paving could be a real jewel – rather like having a Picasso on a wall. Usually the artist will make it on a plastic mesh in a workshop, and when it's finished will move it to site and set it in concrete.

Raised surfaces & earth-mounding

Designer Tips

Making an Earth Mound
It is essential for the side slopes of the mound to be stable. If you plan to grass the surface, the slope needs to be a maximum of 1:3 for easy mowing.

Planting, once established, will usually help to stabilize the soil, but to get it to establish you may need to use special netting (see Suppliers' Guide), which is pegged onto the slope. You can either turf over it or cut slits and plant through it.

In theory, you can stabilize a near-vertical slope this way. In practice, watering is a problem as drainage is ultra-efficient on very steep slopes. The addition of moisture-retaining granules (see Suppliers' Guide) when you plant will help.

It is not necessary to use fine topsoil for the whole mound; the structural shapes can be made of subsoil, or even rubble. What is very important is that you add soil in layers not more than 20cm (8in) thick, compacting each one as you go with a heavy roller. Make sure the soil is dry when you do this, or the soil structure could be damaged. If compaction is not done properly the mount will tend to settle and subside unevenly. The soil will take about 12 months to settle, so start planting only after that. Use this period to kill off all weeds which appear, and if you are going to use netting, put it on now.

RIGHT *This spiralling mound is at The Menagerie in Northamptonshire. The steep slopes are clothed in a continuous drift of* Acaena microphylla, *a creeping evergreen perennial which has bright red burrs in late summer that light up the slopes.*

Huge man-made hills constructed thousands of years ago still create stunning impacts on their immediate environment. On a far less staggering scale, but still forming an exhilarating statement, are the mounts which were popular in the late sixteenth and seventeenth century. These raised areas, usually grassed, were created to form lookout points over the garden – often a particularly interesting part of the garden like an intricate parterre – and beyond. Although these historic examples are on a large scale, the technique can be scaled down for the domestic garden and used to make anything from gentle slopes and dips to amphitheatres and mounded dragons.

Modern earth-moving machinery has been developed and refined so that it is easy to use and very manageable, fitting through even narrow entrance ways, so it is understandable why the technique is increasing in popularity. On a practical note, earth mounds have the added advantage of acting as efficient sound barriers and this is sometimes their primary function. When it comes to selecting a style, earth mounds often channel ideas that are fantastically exhibitionist through the formation of obviously man-made shapes, such as regular spirals, amphitheatres and dragons. Alternatively, earth mounding can be used to create natural hillocks and undulations in keeping with the local landscape. They may also provide an enclosure, a barrier to unwanted noise or simply relief from a very flat terrain.

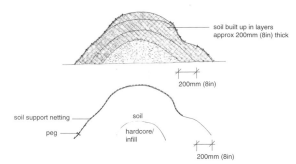

FIG 13 *Earth mound cross-section*

Steps

RIGHT *These steep steps closely follow the profile of the grass bank. Their narrow, almost precipitous feel helps promote an organic quality.*

FAR RIGHT TOP *The pebble risers are an unusual feature and give an organic look to these steps designed by Paul Cooper. This is emphasized by the relatively narrow treads compared to the steep risers.*

FAR RIGHT BELOW *These steps really fit in with their surroundings, giving them a strong organic nature. The roughly hewn stone on the steps, in the walls and in the surrounding beds helps tie in all the elements.*

Changes in level in a garden provide tremendous scope for creating character and interest, sometimes even exhilaration and drama. Steps can be shallow, leisurely and winding, or they may feel precarious, steep and dramatic. They can be grand and formal, topped with urns or statues. They can be hewn into a slope, heavily worn as though they are almost part of the rock itself, or they can be floating, cantilevered structures.

ORGANIC STEPS

Hewn out of rock, sculpted from springy turf or constructed out of timber or logs, these steps are designed to look part of the slope itself. They fit with the landscape rather than imposing an alien character on it.

Steps cut out of the earth, turfed with sloping risers and flat expansive treads of grass, inevitably have a curved sculptural feel to them. Although simple, they can be very dramatic. They usually have narrow risers and the treads are of a generous width, resulting in soft, flowing lines. At Dartington Hall Gardens there are some wonderful grass steps with just these proportions. On a less lavish scale turf steps can still be very eye-catching: mini-terraces with 15cm (6in) battered risers and generous treads of around 1m (3ft 3in) will look quite striking.

Battered Risers

It is important to batter the risers at an angle of about 45–60° to make turf steps stable. Use some proprietary netting under the turf to bind the soil until the grass is

well established. The mowing of the risers is best performed with a strimmer or a hover mower.

If wear-and-tear is a problem, grass steps can flank conventional paved steps, provided these are kept very simple, so as to maintain the flow of easy lines. You could also combine planted risers with paved treads. Use plants that knit closely together, tolerate dry conditions and sprout back if they are kicked around from time to time. *Hedera* species (ivy), *Buxus suffruticosa*

(dwarf box), and carpeting thymes are good choices. It may be a little difficult to get them established because of their awkward position. Use stabilizing netting, as well as moisture-retentive granules incorporated into the soil, and water regularly for the first summer and in dry periods. Alternatively, use turfs folded inside out, make slits and wedge the plants in them. The tread of the step will need to be cantilevered out, and project over the growing medium and plants to ensure a clean edge.

ARCHITECTURAL STEPS

These steps will be closely associated with a building, and so it is important that they reflect and echo its character, both in terms of materials and architectural style. Above and beyond this, there is plenty of scope for excellent design and detailing. Circular steps combined with half circles form an interesting shape, as shown in the photograph above. The use of tiles on end, which easily fit into a curve, form an additional

special detail. Bricks used in tight curves involve a lot of expensive and skilled cutting, in larger circles cutting will not be necessary (see Fig 11, page 71).

Steps may be formed from gentle curves, a half ellipse, a serpentine, half hexagons and as many other geometric and free shapes as are compatible with the overall design. Visually, it is better if steps are much wider than is strictly necessary. This applies particularly in places in which they are adjacent to paved areas and driveways. In these situations they can offer additional seating space as well as providing an interesting focal point.

For theatrical effect, grand, double flights of steps fit the bill. An excellent example of magnificent architectural steps is found at the Villa Garzoni, with its Italian baroque garden, where three double-ramped staircases climb the hill to a fantastic cascade at the top. However, double sets of steps do not have to be on a grand scale. Instead of stone balustrading, one could use simple brick retaining walls with timber fencing. They will still be striking, and more in keeping with most houses and gardens.

ABOVE *The risers on these steps are made from ivy. The most effective way to establish plants in this position is to use small plants on a not quite vertical riser and either stabilize the soil with a proprietary netting or use turfs back to front and slit them to get the plants in. Soak the plants prior to planting and add moisture-retentive granules to the fill.*

ABOVE RIGHT *These Portland stone steps with simple but elegant detailing create a bold, almost circular half landing. They were designed by Tom Stuart-Smith.*

FAR RIGHT *These generously proportioned architectural steps are formed from part circles used to create an almost circular half landing They were designed by Michael Balston.*

RIGHT *The fine, elegantly curving balustrades on these wide steps at the late Sir Clough Williams-Ellis' garden, Plas Brondanw, at Portmeirion, are an essential part of their charm.*

Another way to make a statement is to exaggerate the steepness or shallowness of a flight of steps. For the former use relatively high risers, narrow treads and a narrow overall width. To emphasize the shallowness of a flight of steps, use relatively shallow risers, broad treads and a generous width. Exaggerating elements in this manner usually works better for short flights than for long ones. To exaggerate the steepness of a slope still further, increase the height at the top of the steps by placing some tall plants, huge urns or perhaps a fence at the top. Conversely, to reduce the height of the slope, keep higher elements at the bottom of the flight of steps.

EXHILARATING STEPS
Some steps, through their careful structuring and design, are so detached from the ground that they seem to float. They are exhilarating to use and make fantastically dramatic garden features. One way of achieving the effect is to cantilever the treads out from some adjacent walling. The wall must be substantial enough to take the thrust on the step. The treads may be made of stone, concrete, metal or even hefty sections of wood.

Ladder steps, which again have no risers, also have a light appearance. They can be ideal for tree houses,

decking areas, boat houses and gypsy caravans (see page 88) where it is important for the structure to be apparently detached from ground level. They are as unobtrusive and transparent as possible, to achieve the floating effect. If hand railing is required, it may be possible to use rope, perhaps in conjunction with steel wires to prevent too much movement. Ladder steps are often made of metal, and tie in well with balconies. They are often painted black or dark brown so that they recede into the background, or link with other metal work.

ABOVE RIGHT *Irregular deep risers and narrow treads give the impression that these steps were hewn out of the rock face by natural forces. They encourage a desire to see what is at the top around the corner.*

FAR RIGHT *Steps that lead nowhere make an interesting feature in their own right. Naturalized plants have taken hold here but the steps might also provide a good display area for containers.*

the play element

 **I**F YOU WOULD LIKE A BEAU-
TIFUL GARDEN THAT PRO-
VIDES A TRANQUIL OASIS
WHERE YOU CAN TRULY
RELAX AND ESCAPE THE HUMDRUM
NECESSITIES OF LIFE, BUT THINK IT
WOULD BE IMPOSSIBLE TO ACHIEVE
BECAUSE THE LAWN IS A FOOTBALL
PITCH AND THE BORDERS ARE CONTINU-
ALLY DISTURBED BY BALLS, DOGS AND
TRAMPLING FEET, THEN YOU SHOULD
READ ON. CHILDREN *CAN* BE COM-
PATIBLE WITH STUNNING GARDENS
PROVIDED YOU ARE REALISTIC AND
ALLOW THEM A REASONABLE AMOUNT
OF THEIR OWN SPACE. THE PROVISION
OF A SAFE, OUTDOOR SPACE TO PLAY
SPORT, LET OFF STEAM AND INDULGE IN
FANTASTIC ADVENTURES IS WHAT
CHILDHOOD IS ALL ABOUT. FURTHER-
MORE, IF YOU MAKE 'HONEYPOT AREAS'
TO ENTICE THEM IT WILL LEAVE THE REST
OF THE GARDEN TO THE GARDENERS.

Children's private space

DESIGN 'A HONEYPOT AREA'

To achieve the ideal children's garden you have to explore the possibilities and examine the practicalities. With the children's involvement, you first need to decide what everyone would like and then prioritize your combined needs, pulling them into an overall design. If you have the space, there are undeniable advantages in creating a specific area for the children. This acts as a 'honeypot' enticing them to that area and leaving you to concentrate your horticultural efforts in other, more tranquil spaces.

The honeypot area need not be large but it should have one or more elements which are definitely children-orientated. Theirs to help design and, preferably, make; theirs to alter and amend. This capacity to be changed is fundamental to the area's success, and is partly why I am not particularly keen on off-the-shelf climbing frames and other equipment. Apart from their physical appearance, they are static and do not fully encourage the children to use their imaginative and creative skills.

LOOKING AHEAD

Children like challenges and they develop at such a rate that they are soon bored with the pleasures on offer. As with indoor toys which are changed on a regular basis as new skills and interests are acquired, so too should their garden environment be capable of adaptation, or they will become over-familiar with the equipment and will either not use it or will use it for activities for which it was never intended. More often than not, these activities will be dangerous.

With tailor-made equipment the children have more scope to contribute to its design and development. We have a tree house (see pages 96–102), which evolved from year to year. In the first year, the children insisted on allowing the native cow parsley to grow up all around it. They trod paths through it and made dens within it. Then they purloined a hammock which they hung beneath it. They made and decorated heraldic wooden shields to embellish it. Rope ladders, monkey swings and knotted ropes have subsequently been added.

RIGHT *This children's area is only partially visible from the house, as I've screened it with an open trellis which is colour co-ordinated with the play-house, containing a train set and other items. The playhouse was 'off the shelf' but then painted to tie in with the rest of the garden. The blue/grey finish is Sadolin's Superdec Limestone, which is opaque. This colour works well with stone buildings and is repeated on the doors and windows of the main house.*

Their next project is to have a flying fox which will go from the tree house to a neighbouring tree. When you design and/or make play equipment, bear in mind the possibilities for future development so that additions and other elements can be added. Also bear in mind that any DIY efforts should be made with maximum strength and that safety should be considered the first priority.

CREATING AN ATMOSPHERE

There are many possibilities for play equipment within a children's private garden, but almost as important as the items you and they wish to include is the overall 'feel' of the space. I favour a lush area, with a wild tone to it, perhaps surrounded or entirely composed of dense shrubs, carpeted underneath with groundcover plants and some vigorous and colourful herbaceous flowers. These densely planted areas – which need not be huge – provide privacy for the children, are good at absorbing their paraphernalia and lessen their impact on the rest of the garden. Trees, if there is the space, should be part of their area. If there are none, I would plant a framework comprising *Prunus avium* (wild cherry), *Betula pendula* (birch) or *Fraxinus ornus* (manna ash).

Having decided on your 'woodland' belt, carpeted with ivies, *Vinca*, comfrey and other indestructible groundcovers conducive to secret camps and hideaways, you will find it easier to accommodate other features without encroaching on the more tended areas of garden.

BELOW This homemade rustic football goal also doubles up as a den. I've covered it up with a large camouflage net which I bought from an army surplus store. We also use the net for shading/screening the rabbit run and making temporary dens.

Earth mounding (see page 78) allows you to alter the landscape where you like and therefore proves very useful for defining a children's area or individual features like sandpits. It can also be used to build interesting play features such as amphitheatres, barrows and mounds.

Depending on the amount of space you have, consider introducing a crocodile willow tunnel, a sandpit, a playhouse, a climbing tree, swings, a fort, a wildlife pool, a rill or a gypsy caravan (see page 88).

ESTABLISHING THE PLANTING

Prunus avium, *Betula pendula* and *Fraxinus ornus* will eventually become quite large, but I would still plant them quite densely, perhaps 2m (6ft 6in) or so apart. The aim is not to produce fine specimens but trees that will quickly provide a woodland feel, an air of mystery, dappled shade and ideal den-making country. The canopies will quickly knit together and the trees will form groups with character. Buy young bare-rooted trees 60–90cm (2–3ft) tall because at this small size they transplant well, establish quickly, are inexpensive and will soon overtake a standard tree planted at the same time. Staking will also be unnecessary at this size, even if your garden is exposed.

If your house is close by and these (potentially) forest trees concern you, they can be coppiced at 10-yearly intervals or so. When coppicing, saw them down to just above ground level. This will make them throw up several shoots in response and they will eventually grow into multi-stem trees, which you can cut back again in another 10 years or so.

Don't coppice them all at once, as this would result in a sudden barren appearance. Instead, work your way round the trees, year by year. If your house is built on shrinkable clay and the trees are only 5m (16ft) or so away, then I would stick to large shrubs to avoid subsidence problems. In any case, I would not plant a tree closer to the house than 4m (12ft).

SWINGS

Swings are ever-popular, appealing to a huge age range. However, the swing is also one of the most dangerous pieces of equipment in the play area. The 'swinger' is out of control for much of the time and if other children cut in front of the swing's path, they can be badly hurt. For this reason, avoid the charming wooden seats and the plastic ones, both of which are dangerous on

BELOW LEFT *This willow crocodile is one year old. I made it with long (2–3m/6½–10ft) willow cuttings (Salix viminalis). I mulched the inside with bark. To make the taller arches I used two long cuttings either side and joined them at the top. It requires cutting back and weaving several times during the growing season to prevent the shape becoming lost.*

BELOW RIGHT *This playhouse is made from marine ply and painted with bright colours. It is fairly sizeable – 2.3 × 1.8m (96 × 71in) with a door height of about 1.1m (43in) – and so, in my experience, children will tend to use it until they are about 11 or so. Try to site playhouses in slightly out-of-the-way places, where they are less visible and give the occupants more privacy.*

impact, and choose one made from an impact-absorbing rubber (see Suppliers' Guide). Site the swing in a corner or other place where children will be less likely to meander across the swing line. If at all possible, erect a double swing: it is much more fun swinging with a sibling or friend and you will avoid the inevitable squabbles associated with 'taking turns'.

WILLOW TUNNELS AND FENCES

Willow is a wonderful material for creating interesting structures. By weaving the pliable stems, you can quickly make organic-looking low fences, archways, tunnels, retaining banks or hidey-hole huts (see page 114 for weaving techniques). Tunnels are always fun, particularly for younger children. They are very simple to make using 2–3m (6½–9ft) cuttings of *Salix viminalis* (common osier) – see Suppliers' Guide. Huts, fences and tunnels can be linked to create exciting private spaces which children can adapt and alter when the mood takes them. You can use sand as a surface in and under the tunnels and hut (although if you have a problem with neighbourhood cats, shredded bark may be a better choice).

USING SAND

A large, home-made sandpit can be combined with other items such as log seats, maybe some water, a stepping stone log maze and a tunnel – these will encourage older children to use the sand as well as the younger ones. Several children can work together to construct quite complex features, getting thoroughly absorbed in their endeavours.

Sandpits are easy to construct. Dig a large hole approximately 40cm (1ft 4in) deep and line it with a geotextile membrane (see Suppliers' Guide) Define the edge with large boulders, slabs or log rounds partially sunk into the soil and then fill the hole with sand. If your soil does not drain well you will need to put about 15cm (6in) of free-draining material such as sand beneath the membrane. In extremely soggy conditions you will need to raise the sand above the ground and make a wall of timber, brick or stone to contain it.

Sandpit sand is classified as a toy and is available in small bags. However, for larger quantities it is more economical to buy the sand loose. Light-coloured sand is preferable as it does not stain clothes. Always check that the sand is lime-free. Avoid builders' sand as it does not form decent sandcastles.

PLAYHOUSES

Wendy houses are always a delight to children – both girls and boys. They provide interest over a long period and still appeal even when the children reach 10 or 11. Position the Wendy house in a quiet, private spot, ideally with a tiny garden or perhaps a low fence

ABOVE RIGHT *This low-key play area is comfortably sited at the bottom of an old orchard. A wavy blue slide sits upon a wooden Wendy house with ladder access from the back. Two swings are included, allowing siblings and friends to swing and chat together. The small water feature adds extra play value, encourages wildlife and is shallow enough not to present a hazard.*

RIGHT (FIG 14) *This sketch illustrates how a Judas door can be introduced to make a full-size door more child-friendly. It is a useful way of temporarily transformng a garden shed into a playhouse until it can be reclaimed for adult use.*

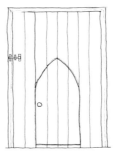

FIG 14 *A Judas door*

around it. However beautifully you make it, most Wendy houses will be improved with planting so that they are partially obscured.

As it will be in use for a good length of time, make sure that the design of the Wendy house is attractive and fulfils what you want it to do. In the early years of childhood, teddies' tea parties will suffice but as the years go by its use will change. If it is big enough to camp in, albeit rather like sardines in a can, a playhouse will provide interest up until the early teens. I used a basic off-the-peg garden shed to form the basis of a gypsy caravan (see page 88) which is ideally suited to this purpose.

Gypsy caravan

Many gardens have a basic prefabricated garden shed. It is often inherited with the house and is not usually a thing of great beauty. My children had been hankering after a gypsy caravan for several years and, as we inherited an unwanted shed, it was decided that a dramatic conversion was in order. Our shed was 2.1m (7ft) by 1.55m (5ft 2in) with a low monopitch roof rising to a height of 2m (6½ft) from a height of 1.85m (6ft 2in) — hardly the proportions of a gypsy caravan as it was too square, but there would just be enough room for bunks for two inside with a little bit of space to spare. The other difficulty with the proposed conversion was that the door was on one side and not at the end. After two days of sawing, hammering and painting we were all pleasantly surprised by the end result and it now forms a much fought-over spare sleeping area when the children have friends to stay.

These dimensions are based on one particular shed and it will be necessary to adapt the design to the size of shed used. If your shed is wider than ours, you should install horizontal beams to support all four sides of the base (see Raising the shed). See page 94 for materials list.

RAISING THE SHED

The area was prepared to take the shed by firming four posts, 720 × 150 × 150mm (2ft 4¾in × 6in × 6in), into holes in the ground to a depth of 300mm (12in) which were then back-filled with well-rammed excavated material. The posts were positioned in a square with 1.15m (3ft 10in) between the posts on all sides. One post was set to the correct height and then, taking this as a datum point, the other posts were all set level with it using a spirit level and a straight-edged length of timber across the post tops.

The two horizontal beams, 2.1m × 200mm × 70mm (7ft × 8in × 2¾in), were laid flat side down on top of the posts and centred on them, so that they were parallel to each other and parallel to the proposed front elevation of the shed. These were fixed into position using two roundhead nails on each post. The shed was positioned on top of the beams and fixed by screwing through the base bearers of the shed into the beams with 75mm (3in) screws.

To support a wider shed, you should fit beams under the end walls as well. Install two additional posts at each end, 25mm (1in) in from the ends of the long beams and 100mm (4in) away from them, and fit a short

1 | *Raising the shed on posts added height to the original squat structure and provided fixing positions for the wheels. It is essential that the shed base is firmly supported to withstand the inevitable activity inside the caravan and the weight of the occupants and furniture. Additional end beams should be installed for sheds wider than ours.*

1

used to describe and mark the circle. The centre of the curve (its highest point) was marked by drawing a line at right-angles from the centre of the baseline, to assist in positioning the ridge beam later. The semi-circles were then cut out with a jigsaw.

To provide support for the canvas along the length of the shed, two 125mm (5in) wide-curved formers were used. The outer curve was marked on the ply as before, at a 1100mm (3ft 8in) radius from the centre of a 1640mm (5ft 5½in) long baseline. Then, using the same centre, a second curve was marked inside the first one at a radius 125mm (5in) smaller than before, that is 975mm (3ft 3in). The centre of the curve was also marked, and the formers were cut out with a jigsaw.

The end panels were attached to the frame of the shed using two screws at each end and two in the middle. The semi-circles were positioned at the lowest height possible where they covered the highest top corner of the existing shed roof so that the roof outline would be totally concealed under the canvas. The lower part of the vertical edges were cut flush with the feather-edged boards in order to allow a good fixing for the fascia boards.

The two curved formers were held flush against the end panels and the angle of the shed roof was marked on the bottom ends; the ends were then cut off to this angle. Next, a 25mm (1in) wide notch was cut in the centre of the outer curve of each of the formers to a depth of 50mm (2in) so that they could be connected flush with the ridge beam.

The ridge beam was formed from a batten measuring 2.1m × 75 × 25mm (7ft × 3 × 1in). Two notches 12mm (½in wide) by 25mm (1in) deep were cut in one edge, centred 700mm (2ft 4in) from each end. The ridge beam was then slotted on to the formers and positioned between the two end panels. It was screwed to the end panel at each end, and the formers were screwed on the angle into the shed roof.

A green canvas tarpaulin measuring 3.65 × 2.75m (12 × 9ft), obtained from the local builders' merchant, was then positioned centrally over the roof. The ropes were left attached for the time being to help with positioning it. The ends of the tarpaulin were gathered in pleats at each end of the shed and tacked on to the ply board using felting nails. When all was secure, the ropes were cut through the spliced end to remove them.

FITTING THE FASCIAS

At both ends of the shed above the centre of the fascia board there was a gap where the tacking of the ends of the tarpaulin was not hidden. An approximate semi-circle with a base of 350mm (1ft 2in) and a radius of 220mm (8¾in), cut in the same way as the other ones from the plywood, was fixed with roundhead nails over the gap.

Four fascia boards were cut out from 150 × 20mm (6 × ¾in) timber boards. Two were about 1650mm (5ft 6in) long and two about 2200mm (7ft 4in) long. The long ones were cut to length after the end ones had been fixed so that they fitted snugly between them.

The curved pattern for the lower edge of the fascia boards was marked out using a template. You can make your own template on a length of felt paper. Draw a line parallel to one edge and 225mm (9in) from it. Mark

8| *Cut the ends of the curved formers to the angle of the shed roof and cut notches in the formers and ridge beam so that the top edges lie flush. Position this assembly with the ridge beam butting up to the centre marks on the end panels and screw it in position. Pre-drill the screw holes in the edge of the formers to avoid splitting the plywood.*

9| *Unroll the tarpaulin to its full length and centre it on the ridge beam so that an equal amount is hanging over each end. Then unroll half the width and work your way back to your access ladder while unrolling the second half. From below, you can then make final adjustments to the position, using the ropes to help you if necessary.*

10| *Pleat the ends of the tarpaulin over the end panels. Start by bringing the middle of the end of the tarpaulin down so that it lies parallel to the base of the end panel, and tack this part into position with felting nails. Then work towards the edges, folding and tacking each section as you progress. Cut through the spliced loops of the ropes to remove them.*

every 225mm along the line and draw a 225mm radius semi-circle from each mark, to give a series of overlapping curves. Repeat this procedure on another piece of paper using 75mm (3in) units for the small 'shield' shapes. Cut these out and tape them securely in position centrally between the larger overlapping curves so that the point of the 'shield' is at the edge of the paper. Finally cut along the outline.

The height of all four fascia boards was fixed so that the bottom edge of the fascia board above the windows would be 25mm (1in) above the inner edge of the top window frame member. Two nails were tapped into each wall of the shed to rest the fascia boards on while they were screwed into position. The shorter fascia boards were fixed to each end of the shed on the ply semi-circle by screwing through the ply into the upright supports with two screws at each end and in the middle. The remaining two fascia boards were fixed along the sides of the shed, taking care to conceal the edges of the tarpaulin behind them, by screwing through into the uprights inside the shed.

Window fascias were cut from 30 × 15mm (1¼ × ⅝in) beading – two 760mm (2ft 6½in) lengths and two 360mm (1ft 2½in) lengths for each window, with a 45 degree mitre at each end. They were nailed round the outside of each window, flush with the inside of the window frame; the top window fascias were tucked just behind the roof fascia board. Two fillets of timber measuring 700 × 32 × 10mm (2ft 4in × 1¼ × ⅜in) were then nailed to the vertical inside edges of each window to cover the small gaps between the feather-edged boards and the beading.

PROVIDING ACCESS

The two ladder side rails were 1425mm (4ft 9in) long and cut from 100mm deep by 50mm wide (4 × 2in) timber. The ends were sawn at 45 degrees so that they were parallel to the shed wall at the top and to the ground at the bottom. They were positioned 400mm (1ft 4in) apart and set about 50mm (2in) into the soil – so that the top of the ladder just reached to the bottom of the door opening. If the soil is soft, excavate two holes about 150mm (6in) deep, stand the feet of the ladder on 100mm (4in) of well-rammed coarse aggregate and backfill with aggregate round them.

The side rails were fixed at the top with two screws on the angle through the feather-edged boarding into two support posts. These posts were cut from 70 × 40mm (2¾ × 1⅝in) timber to fit vertically between the bottom door frame trimmers and the shed base bearer, so as to give extra support to the door threshold. They were screwed on the angle at the top and bottom, flat against the shed wall. Four rungs, 60 × 40mm (2⅜ × 1⅝in), with the top edges rounded with a plane to make them easier to grasp, were fixed with two screws at each end to the side rails at approximately 300mm (12in) centres.

Adding the wheels

Imitation wheels were improvised from four sections of a Cambridge roller (an agricultural machine) which were retrieved from a scrap yard. These are 540mm (1ft 9in) in diameter. Alternatively, they could be cut out from a sheet of exterior ply or adapted from some other suitable wheel.

11| *After cutting the fascia boards to length, position your template along one edge and adjust the position along the length of the fascia board to give a balanced result to the pattern. Tape the template to the plywood and mark along the outline of the curves with a pencil, then cut out the curves with a jigsaw, working into the angles from both directions.*

12| *Set the height of the side fascia board above the windows, before resting the end fascias on supporting nails and fixing them in position with long screws. The small semi-circle of ply is covering the bare centre of the end panel. Cut the side fascias to fit snugly between the end ones and screw them to the edges of the end panels and the curved formers.*

13| *To give the windows a more finished appearance, cut fascias from a length of beading and mitre the ends at 45 degrees. The distance between the inside corners of the mitres is the inside dimension of the window frame. Fix the fascias to the window frame with oval wire nails and punch the heads below the surface with a nail punch.*

Because the metal 'wheels' we used had hollow centres, axles were cut from dowel rod and screwed on to 40mm (1⅝in) thick timber spacers measuring 70 × 70mm (2¾ × 2¾in). These in turn were fixed to the vertical posts supporting the shed, with the centre of the dowel 270mm (10½in) above the ground. A wheel boss was cut for each wheel from a waste piece of turned timber to fit over the hollow centre and was screwed on to the axle to secure the wheel.

PAINTING THE CARAVAN

The caravan was painted using an opaque woodstain for all the timber work and a matt exterior-grade paint (over a primer and undercoat) for the wheels. The woodstains used were from the Sadolin Superdec range, with Clover Leaf for all the main areas, Rose Smoke to pick out the barge boards and other areas, and Fali Straw for the windows.

14| *The tops of the ladder rails were fixed to supporting posts inside the shed wall which were in turn screwed to the door trimmers and shed base bearer. Screw the rungs to the rails with at least 225mm (9in) clearance between them, to avoid any danger of children becoming trapped. The top rung should lie just below the door threshold.*

15| *These wheels had a hollow centre and were mounted on non-loadbearing dowel axles, so the weight of the wheels must rest on the ground! Screw the axles to timber spacers and mount these on the support posts. Then position the wheels and secure them with wheel bosses screwed on to the end of the axles.*

Materials List

Shed: 2.1 × 1.55m (7ft × 5ft 2in)
Posts: 4 no. 720 × 150 × 150mm (2ft 4¾in × 6in × 6in)
Horizontal beams: 2 no. 2.1m × 200mm × 70mm (7ft × 8in × 2¾in)

WINDOWS
Vertical posts: 2 no. 1.85m × 50mm × 27mm (6ft 2in × 2in × 1in)
Top and bottom frame members: 4 no. 300 × 50 × 27mm (1ft × 2in × 1in)
Glazing bars:
2 no. 700 × 18 × 18mm (2ft 4in × ¾in × ¾in)
4 no. 300 × 18 × 18mm (1ft × ¾in × ¾in)
Window fascias:
4 no. 760 × 30 × 15mm (2ft 6½in × 1¼in × ⅝in) beading
4 no. 360 × 30 × 15mm (1ft 2½in × 1¼in × ⅝in) beading
Vertical fillets: 4 no. 700 × 32 × 10mm (2ft 4in × 1¼in × ⅜in)
Glazing: 2 no. 700 × 300 × 3mm (2ft 4in × 1ft × ⅛in) Perspex sheet

DOOR
Vertical posts: 2 no. 2.1m × 50mm × 27mm (7ft × 2in × 1in)
Trimmers: 4 no. 386 × 50mm × 27mm (1ft 3½in × 2in × 1in)
Subframe:
2 no. 1100 × 40 × 35mm (3ft 8in × 1⅝in × 1⅜in)
2 no. 800 × 40 × 35mm (2ft 8in × 1⅝in × 1⅜in)
Feather-edged boards: 11 no. 800 × 115 × 12mm (2ft 8in × 4⅝in × ½in) – or reuse the existing ones
Swivel catch: 63 × 32 × 25mm (2½ × 1¼ × 1in)
Hook-and-eye door clasp

ROOF
End panels and formers: 2 sheets of 2400 × 1200 × 12mm (8ft × 4ft × ½in) exterior-grade plywood (WBP)
Ridge beam: 1 no. 2.1m × 75mm × 25mm (7ft × 3in × 1in)
Green canvas tarpaulin 3.65 × 2.75m (12 × 9ft)
Fascia boards:
2 no. 1.65m × 150mm × 20mm (5ft 6in × 6in × ¾in)
2 no. about 2.2m × 150mm × 20mm (7ft 4in × 6in × ¾in)

LADDER
Side rails: 2 no. 1425 × 100 × 50mm (4ft 9in × 4in × 2in)
Rungs 4 no. 500 × 60 × 40mm (1ft 8in × 2⅜in × 1⅝in)
Support posts: 2 no. approximately 400 × 70 × 40mm (2ft 8in × 2¾in × 1⅝in) – to fit between shed base bearer and trimmers

Notes:
All timber is planed-all-round (PAR), tannelized softwood, except where stated.
Use either metric or imperial measurements but not a mixture of the two.

WHEELS

4 sections of a Cambridge agricultural roller

Spacers: 4 no. 70 × 70 × 40mm (2¾ × 2¾ × 1⅝in)

Axles: 4 no. 38mm (1½in) diameter dowel (length to match wheel thickness)

Wheel bosses: 4 no. 50mm (2in) long sections of turned timber (to cover centre of wheels)

SCREWS AND NAILS

50 and 75mm (2 and 3in) × No. 8 zinc-plated counter-sunk head woodscrews

12mm (½in) × No. 4 roundhead screws

40 and 125mm (1½ and 5in) roundhead nails

32mm (1¼in) oval wire nails, felting nails

Non-setting mastic

Opaque woodstain, such as Sadolin Superdec range. Colours used were: Clover Leaf (main areas); Rose Smoke (roof boards, ladder and base beams); Fali Straw (window fascias).

Metal primer, undercoat and matt exterior-grade top coat (for wheels)

TOOLS

Spade, shovel, spirit level, jigsaw, panel saw, Surform plane or rasp, tenon saw, electric drill, 4mm (⁵⁄₃₂in) drill bit, drill bits for screws, countersink, G-cramps, screwdriver, hammer, nail punch, plane, frame gun (for mastic cartridge).

CABLE RUNWAYS

A cable runway or 'flying fox' is one of the most exhilarating pieces of play equipment. It is a relatively unobtrusive construction consisting only of a long length of rope fixed from one high point to another with a pulley attached. Tree houses or raised timber platforms are suitable launching places to fix the ends of the rope.

When you fix the two high end points of rope, make sure they are positioned high enough to provide a clear sweep under the rope for the child to swing without touching the ground. One end of the rope must be fixed in such a way that the child is able to climb up and get hold of the pulley. At the other end you can arrange the height so that it is slightly lower, enabling the child to jump off easily. See Suppliers' Guide for pulley suppliers.

GENERAL LANDSCAPING

Grassy knolls and sculpted mounds can provide partial enclosure or elevated lumps and bumps which children can enjoy cycling, running and jumping up and over. On a smaller scale, a low grassy mound partially enclosing a sandpit enables children to exploit the area for other, non-sand purposes. A tiny amphitheatre formed from earth with grass steps could be used as a quiet, sheltered spot to read alone or it could become an outside stage when other children are around. On a slightly larger scale, a sweeping serpentine grass mound could be designed as an interesting element that also separates the children's area from an ornamental stretch of lawn.

RIGHT *This is a cable runway or flying fox. It was made by TP Toys (see Suppliers' Guide) and is fixed, in this instance, at one end to a tree house and the other end to an apple tree. Visually it forms little impact on the garden, but it contributes hugely to the play value.*

Tree houses

Tree houses make the ideal addition to a children's garden, providing an elevated hideaway where they can see you but you can't see them. They will play quite happily for hours in such lofty places, surrounded by bird song and rustling, camouflaging leaves.

The structure hidden in the tree may be above eye level, so it will be partially screened and not as intrusive as it would be if it were at ground level. Tree houses are ideal places to create fantasy worlds and are easily adapted to a variety of different make-believe themes.

ACCOMMODATING A TREE HOUSE

It is not essential to have an old tree with branches conveniently spaced in order to accommodate a tree house. Although these trees do undoubtedly lend themselves to superb tree houses, they tend to be massive, giving rise to a platform height several metres off the ground which is unsuitable for youngsters.

The majority of tree houses I design are virtually or completely free-standing but still incorporated into the tree canopy. This gives you more scope for selecting an appropriate height. For young children, or children who have not developed their co-ordination and agility, it is wise to keep the platform at or below 1.8m (6ft), although even this would be dangerous for very young children without constant parental supervision.

A FREESTANDING TREE HOUSE

There are several different ways to accommodate a tree house. The most common way that I have used is to build a freestanding house set in the canopy of an older tree which is not going to grow much more. To fit it in I have straddled the house over a main branch or contained a branch within the house, the latter looking most picturesque from outside with a branch growing out through the roof. More often than not this method has involved removing one or two minor limbs.

The supporting posts can be camouflaged by dark woodstain and by growing climbers up them or woodland shrubs around them. By using the latter you can create a shady shrubbery underneath the tree house which is highly conducive to turning into a lower-level den. Choose shrubs which will shoot back when trodden on and tolerate a dry spot in dappled shade. *Corylus avellana* (hazel), the larger cotoneasters, *Prunus laurocerasus* (laurel) and *Viburnum lantana* (the wayfaring tree) are useful in this situation.

Other methods I have seen involve constructing a house between two, three or four adjacent trees. Sometimes the number of posts required make it virtually self-supporting. Building the house around the trunk, thereby creating a circular structure and supporting the inside on the trunk and the outside on supporting posts, is another possibility. If you have to make fixings on the tree, the occasional screw into the tree is often a better solution than using rope to secure the structure. This may seem strange, but in a few months rope can start to affect the tree adversely if it is tightly fixed, and your very good intentions about loosening the rope at regular intervals will usually have been forgotten.

The larger apple and pear trees are ideal for supported structures and oaks and cherry trees are often a popular choice. Avoid trees such as *Robinia pseudoacacia* (false acacia) and horse chestnut which grow very fast and have a tendency to shed limbs with little advance notice. Obviously a healthy tree without signs of rot and decay is a good start, although it will not matter if an older tree suffers from a bit of dieback.

With all play equipment, accidents tend to happen at the points where children climb in and out or on and off. Make sure the access points are as safe as possible. For young children, wooden steps complete with a handrail on both sides improves safety.

A ladder should be positioned at a stable angle, around 60°. The rungs should be curved on the top edges to encourage a good strong grip. Consider putting a safety surface under the ladder such as bark or sand (see page 86). Finally, do not allow the house to be used unsupervised until you are happy that your children can use it confidently and safely.

Design the tree house to look enticing and fun. A pitched roof will improve the appearance, or if the roof has to be flat make some plywood castellations to go around the edges. Use light materials such as softwood instead of hardwood, perhaps making a basic frame and cladding it with painted plywood, timber boarding or eye-catching fencing. Alternatively, paint it to look like stone (see page 31).

The roof could be covered with a thatch (see page 100), timber shingles or brushwood fixed on with wire. Barge boards, finials, heavy rope, flags and heraldic shields all are simple additions which make the tree house look really special.

Children's tree house

RIGHT *Not having a tree with wide, spreading branches large enough to take a platform, we built this freestanding version which is tucked into the canopy of an old apple tree. We tried to find the best position for the house to minimize the damage to the canopy and root system of the tree, while at the same time ensuring that the structure would look part of the tree. If you do find that you inflict some damage to the roots, you can help the tree recover by watering it in dry periods during the growing season.*

SETTING OUT THE POSTS & PLATFORM

To help work out exactly where the optimum position for the house would be, we used four long lathes of wood as dummies for the four load-bearing posts – one at each corner of the structure. We decided on a rectangular platform 1.4 × 1.2m (4ft 8in × 4ft) and fixed the height at 1.9m (6ft 4in), over a branch. However, young children will need continual supervision at this height. The height allowed room for the branch to grow a bit more without distorting the tree house or harming the branch. It is much safer to choose a healthy older tree than one that is growing vigorously.

The load-bearing posts are 3.8m (12ft 8in) long and 200 × 75mm (8 × 3in), made of tannelized softwood. The bottom 700mm (2ft 4in) was to be set in the ground, leaving the tops 3.1m (10ft 4in) above ground to support the roof. This would give a clearance of 1.2m (4ft) between the platform and the base of the roof, which is adequate for children. The posts are a substantial size so, in order to minimize their visual impact, we positioned them so that the 75mm face (as opposed to their 200mm face) is seen when viewed from the most prominent elevation. We arranged them with the outer corners coinciding with the corners of the platform and the wider face running along the length of the rectangle.

MAKING THE PLATFORM

In our ground conditions we fixed the posts using well-rammed coarse aggregate, but it might well be necessary to use a concrete foundation to surround each post base. Luckily, we only disturbed one small tree root in the process.

To support the platform we used two horizontal base beams, 100 × 50mm (4 × 2in), each spanning two vertical posts and screwed into a housing in the narrow edge of each post. The bottom of each housing was 1.675m (5ft 7in) above the ground – 225mm (9in) below the final height of the platform. Three 100 × 50mm (4 × 2in) horizontal crossbeams were then fixed on top of these base beams, at right-angles to them, to support the floorboards. The two outer crossbeams were screwed to the inner face of the posts; the central one was screwed at an angle from both sides into the base beams.

The floor was made from 177 × 25mm (7 × 1in) boards nailed at right-angles to the crossbeams. The two outermost boards butted up to the inner wide face of the main posts; the remaining boards were cut flush with the outer wide face of the posts. A 3mm (⅛in) gap between the boards allows drainage of any inblown rain and prevents them from warping when wet.

To conceal and protect the ends of the crossbeams, we cut two fascia boards from 12mm (½in) exterior-grade ply using a jigsaw. These were fixed with the top edge flush with the underside of the floorboards, and screwed to the posts and base beams and to the ends of the centre crossbeam.

ERECTING THE BALUSTRADE

We fixed the height of the balustrade at 750mm (2ft 6in), but for adult use this would be too low. It was made from a mixed bunch of leftover sample pickets, which had also been used for testing colours – hence their variety of colour and shape! These were screwed

2| *We used four long lathes of wood to find the optimum position for the posts, then set the posts 700mm (2ft 4in) into the ground and rammed coarse aggregate around them. A batten pinned across the first two posts at platform height was used as a levelling guide. Check that the posts are vertical with a spirit level.*

3| *We wanted to make sure that some of the canopy obscured part of the house on all sides but it was still necessary to remove some branches to accommodate the house. Ideally, the tree house should look like part of the tree and not like a bolted-on extra, but it is also important to minimize damage to the tree.*

1| *None of the trees in our garden was an ideal shape for a traditional tree house, which should fit snugly into wide-spreading limbs. We chose this mature cooking apple tree and decided to build a freestanding tree house supported on posts. We located it over a branch, leaving sufficient clearance for growth.*

at the top and bottom to 75 × 50mm (3 × 2in) horizontal rails which we had fixed all the way round the perimeter (even across the entrance). The top rails were cut to half their thickness at each end and screwed into 75mm (3in) wide by 25mm (1in) deep housings cut 600mm (2ft) above the platform in the outer faces of the main posts. The bottom rails were screwed flat to the floor on all four sides, flush with the edges and ends of the boards.

At the entrance side and the back of the balustrade, the pickets stood on top of the fascias. On the other two sides they were cut 10mm (about ½in) longer so as to project just below the ends of the floorboards and give them some protection from the weather. A gap was left free of pickets at the entrance. Here we placed two extra posts, 75 × 75mm (3 × 3in) – one each side of the entrance – where the top of the ladder was to be fixed. The posts were fixed to the top and bottom balustrade rails by screwing through halving joints.

MAKING THE LADDER

The ladder was made with two 2.4m (8ft) parallel rails, 100 × 50mm (4 × 2in), positioned 450mm (18in) apart. The rungs were 75 × 40mm (3 × 1½in) – a convenient size and shape for children to grip. The ladder was long enough to be positioned at an angle of 60° to the ground. To support the base of the rails and provide drainage in wet weather, coarse aggregate was rammed into the ground beneath them to a depth of 300mm (12in).

The tops of the ladder rails were notched over the platform and bottom balustrade rail, using a bird's-mouth joint. They were screwed to the two entrance posts and, at an angle, into the rail just above and below the joint. The rungs were screwed on to the rails and, to get a good rounded top, we planed off the top edges. The size of the gap between the rungs is critical as they can become traps if too small, so we made ours 250mm (10in) apart.

MAKING THE ROOF FRAMEWORK

We made the roof on the ground first, before fixing it into position. The base was made from four lengths of wood, 75 × 30mm (3 × 1¼in), fixed together at the corners with halving joints to form a rectangle. It was designed to fit on top of the four main posts, flush with the outer faces, and with one of the gable ends over the entrance.

Four rafters were cut from 50 × 40mm (2 × 1½in) timber and the ends were cut to 45°. Two were fixed at each end of the rectangle, at 45° to the roof base, by nailing into the corners of the base. At the top they were nailed to a ridge beam of 150 × 25mm (6 × 1in) timber which connected the two ends. Exterior grade 12mm (½in) ply was screwed to the framework to clad the two roof sides. The final length of each side of the roof was 1.4m (4ft 8in).

Curved barge boards, cut from ply, added a decorative touch and helped to keep the thatch in place. They were screwed to the rafters with the top edge 100mm (4in) proud of the roof boards so as to form an upstand for the thatch to rest against. The bottom edge projected below the rafters. The apex of the gable ends was adorned with a plywood shield to hide the join between the barge boards.

4| *In order to reduce the visual impact of the four main posts we set them with the narrow face towards the entrance and planed off all four corners. The chamfered corners also reduce the risk of injury. To further soften their appearance we later stained them and then concealed them with climbers.*

5| *Two horizontal base beams were set into housing joints in the four main posts and firmly screwed in place. The height of the platform was to be 1.9m (6ft 4in) above the ground, so the bottom of the housing was cut 225mm (9in) below this height, to allow for the thickness of both sets of beams and the floorboards.*

6| *We used some leftover sample pickets for the balustrade. Picket fencing comes in a good range, with different-shaped tops that can be made more eye-catching by your choice of colour. There is great scope for the design of the balustrade, but make sure that it is strong and safe and doesn't encourage children to climb it.*

THATCHING THE ROOF

A traditional thick straw thatch would have been far more expensive than the sedge thatch we used and, because straw thatch is extremely heavy, it would probably have had to be done *in situ*. The thatching on the hut is purely decorative, as the ply is the waterproof element. Instead of thatching the roof, the ply could be clad with timber shingles or wooden lapped boarding, or just stained.

To thatch the roof we used 18 bundles of sedge, with nine bundles thatching each side (see Suppliers' Guide). The bundles were soaked in water for 24 hours to make the thatch pliable. Sedge has sharp edges, so extreme care should be taken when handling it. For this reason it is inadvisable to let the children help with this part of the work.

Two metal rods, 5mm (⅕in) in diameter, were cut to fit along the 1.4m (4ft 8in) length of each side of the roof to hold the thatch in place, and temporarily tied in position near the top and bottom of each roof board. The bundles of sedge were laid under the rods on one side, parallel to the barge boards, and then over the apex of the roof and tucked under the top metal rod on the other side.

As we positioned each bundle we secured it near each metal rod using a 12mm (½in) screw with two wires, about 300mm (1ft) long, attached just under the head. The screw was fixed into the ply and then the two wires were tied round the bundle and the adjacent rod, leaving the overhanging sedge to be tied in with the other side.

We secured the wires with an implement for tying potato sacks, but neat and secure twisting is just as effective if you have not got access to one. We then proceeded to do the other side in the same manner, but tucked under the overlapping thatch from the first side. We then went back to the first side and tucked the overhang from the second side under an additional metal rod positioned a little higher up the roof.

To hide the rods we obtained some heavy natural rope from a chandler's shop and laid a double length of this over each of the exposed rods, fixing it with 10mm (4in) lengths of wire twisted round the rods and the rope. Finally, we trimmed the sedge thatch bundles which overhung the edge to make them look a bit neater. An easier route, if you have a thatcher locally, would be to take the timber roof to a thatcher who would do this part for you.

Having finished the roof, the most awkward part of the job was lifting it up on to the top of the posts – which needed the combined efforts of three adults. Once the roof was positioned on the posts, it was fixed very firmly in place by screwing through the base at an angle into the post tops.

PAINTING THE HOUSE

Finally, we painted the structure with a range of complementary woodstains (see Suppliers' Guide). We used a dark green colour for the main structure and the ladder, and then lightened up the green for the balustrading and barge boards. You could go one shade lighter still for the barge boards in order to make the roof blend in more with the tree. The finishing touch was to add finials to the entrance posts and to paint them red.

7| *The pickets were firmly screwed at top and bottom to horizontal rails. The end 75mm (3in) of the four top rails was cut to half the thickness and screwed into 25mm (1in) deep housings in the four main posts. The base rails were screwed on to the floor, butting up to the posts. Pickets were also fixed to the posts.*

8| *The access points are the most likely places for accidents. The rungs should be a convenient size for children to grip. To achieve this we rounded off the top edges with a plane. Do not put the rungs too close together or they will become potential traps. A good angle for the ladder is about 60 degrees.*

9| *The roof framework needs to be light so that it can be lifted up on to the four post tops when complete. The exterior grade ply made the roof weathertight, leaving the thatch to be purely decorative. The angle of the roof needs to be 45 degrees or more to aid drainage and so help preserve the thatch.*

Notes:
All timber is planed-all-round (PAR), tannelized softwood, except where stated. Use either metric or imperial measurements but not a mixture of the two.

Materials List

PLATFORM

Load-bearing posts: 4 no. 3.8m × 200mm × 75mm
(12ft 8in × 8in × 3in)

Horizontal base beams: 2 no. 1.2m × 100mm × 50mm
(4ft × 4in × 2in)

Horizontal cross beams: 3 no. 1.4m × 100mm × 50mm
(4ft 8in × 4in × 2in)

Floor: 8 no. 1.2m × 175mm × 25mm (4ft × 7in × 1in) –
1 cut to fit on the width, 2 cut to fit on the length

Fascia boards: 2 no. from exterior grade ply,
1.2m × 230mm × 12mm (4ft × 9in × ½in)

BALUSTRADE

Top horizontal rails:

Front and back: 2 no. 1.2m × 75mm × 50mm (4ft × 3in × 2in)

Sides: 2 no. 1.15m × 175mm × 50mm (3ft 10in × 3in × 2in)

Bottom horizontal rails:

Front and back: 2 no. 1.05m × 75mm × 50mm
(3ft 6in × 3in × 2in)

Sides: 2 no. 1m × 75mm × 50mm (3ft 4in × 3in × 2in)

Pickets:

Front and back: 16 no. 775 × 50 × 20mm
(2ft 7in × 2in × ¾in)

Sides: 28 no. 785 × 50 × 20mm (2ft 7½in × 2in × ¾in)

Extra support posts for balustrade: 2 no. 710 × 75 × 75mm
(2ft 4⅛in × 3in × 3in) with post caps, and ball finials
75mm (3in) diameter

LADDER

Parallel rails: 2 no. 2.4m × 100mm × 50mm (8ft × 4in × 2in)

Rungs: 7 no. 550 × 75 × 40mm (1ft 10in × 3in × 1½in)

ROOF

Base frame:

2 no. 1.4m × 75mm × 30mm (4ft 8in × 3in × 1¼in)

2 no. 1.2m × 75mm × 30mm (4ft × 3in × 1¼in)

Rafters: 4 no. 830 × 50 × 40mm (2ft 9¼in × 2in × 1½in)

Ridge beam: 1 no. 1.4m × 150mm × 25mm (4ft 8in × 6in × 1in)

Roof sides: 2 no. sheets of exterior grade, 12mm (½in)
plywood, 1.4m × 820mm (4ft 8in × 2ft 8¼in)

Barge boards: 4 no. from exterior grade, 12mm (½in)
plywood, 1.08m × 230mm (3ft 7in × 9in)

18 bundles of sedge thatch

5 no. 5mm (⅛in) dia. metal rods, 1.4m (4ft 8in) long

30m (100ft) of 0.5mm (⅛₀in) diameter galvanized wire

12m (40ft) of 12mm diameter (1½in circumference)
natural hemp rope

13| *The rope is a purely decorative feature, and is used here to conceal the metal rods which are keeping the bundles of thatch in place. It is readily available from chandler's shops. A double length of rope was used to cover each exposed rod and was fixed to the rod with wire at each end and at intervals of about 150mm (6in).*

10| *The gable ends are made from exterior grade ply cut with a jigsaw. They were screwed to the rafters so as to project 100mm (4in) above them. There is great scope for more elaborate barge boards, perhaps with patterned holes in them. Have a look at some fairy story books for inspiration!*

11| *The bundles of thatch were laid on the ply and fixed by the Dutch method (using metal rods, and screws with wires attached). The screws were fastened into the ply, and then the wires were wrapped round the thatch bundle and the horizontal metal rods. They were tied with a potato sack fastener or twisted with pliers.*

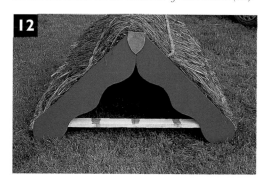

12| *Two metal rods were used on each side of the roof to secure the thatch, and a fifth rod anchored the overhanging thatch from the second side of the roof. This was fixed slightly higher up the roof than the other upper rod (as shown by the position of the rope on the right-hand side of the photo).*

Screws and nails:
25, 40 and 50mm (1, 1½ and 2in) × No.8 zinc-plated
countersunk head woodscrews
75 and 100mm (3 and 4in) × No.10 zinc-plated counter-
sunk head woodscrews
12mm (½in) × No. 6 zinc-plated roundhead woodscrews
25 and 50mm (1 and 2in) oval wire nails

Coarse aggregate, or concrete mix 1:6 (cement:ballast):
approx. 0.5 cu m (0.7 cu yd)

Opaque woodstain, such as Sadolin Superdec range.
Colours used were: Ponderosa Pine (dark green); Rain
Forest (mid-green); Brickwork (red finials)

TOOLS
Portable work bench, steel measuring tape, spade,
shovel, tree saw, spirit level, power drill, high-speed
wood drill bit, drill bits, hammer, screwdriver, try
square, combination square, panel saw or circular saw,
tenon saw, wood plane, chisel, mallet, hacksaw, file,
pliers, handyman's knife.

Other tree houses

ABOVE RIGHT *This tropical tree house sits on stilts in a mourouc tree (Erythrina corallodendrum). Note the deep overhang on the roof to protect the inmates from the heavy rainfall.*

RIGHT *This tree house was designed and built by Richard Foxcroft (see Suppliers' Guide). The walls are made from oak boarding and the roof is made from oak shakes. Shakes are different from shingles in that they are split along the grain of the wood. This means that they are more durable and do not twist and move in the way that shingles are prone to do.*

ABOVE *This is a flying saucer which was designed and made by Richard Foxcroft (see Suppliers' Guide). Its circular shape is made from woven laths of oak. It needs to be suspended from a high branch with ropes to enable it to generate a wide swinging motion. They are made with built-in trays for drinks and/or food and will accommodate more than one person. They are a fantastic asset for both adults' and children's gardens.*

RIGHT *An unusual and colourful treehouse designed and built by Ben Wilson (see Suppliers' Guide). The stained glass windows are a charming detail and the inclusion of the lower storey adds to its play value. It is all constructed from salvaged material.*

plants

PLANTS CAN BE USED TO CREATE AN INFINITE RANGE OF STUNNING SPECIAL EFFECTS. THE VERSATILITY OF THEIR PLIANT GROWING STEMS MEANS THAT THEY CAN BE PLANTED, TRAINED AND SHAPED IN MANY DIFFERENT WAYS. THEY ARE IDEAL FOR PROVIDING THE STRONG ELEMENTS OF GREEN ARCHITECTURE WHICH SO OFTEN PULL A GARDEN TOGETHER. THESE ELEMENTS, WHETHER THEY ARE HEDGES, TOPIARY, GROUPS OF STANDARD PLANTS, PARTERRES, PLEACHED AVENUES OR ARBOURS, CAN BE MANIPULATED TO PROVIDE WHOLLY INDIVIDUAL FEATURES. THERE IS HUGE SCOPE FOR ORIGINALITY IN THIS AREA, SO BE BOLD AND EXPERIMENT WITH PRUNING AND CUTTING REGIMES TO CREATE SOMETHING DIFFERENT. YOU NEED PATIENCE TO SEE THE FRUITS OF YOUR LABOURS, SO GET STARTED AS SOON AS POSSIBLE.

Topiary

ABOVE *Topiary is extremely adaptable, working with both traditional designs and the ultra-modern. These repeating shapes of clipped box and yew create a clean, dramatic geometric design.*

TOP RIGHT (FIG 15)
Hedges can be clipped into an infinite range of shapes and styles — to allow glimpses through, to echo the architecture, to repeat a pattern used elsewhere or simply to embellish. Do not forget the possibilities of planting them in alternative arrangements to the ubiquitous straight line — a serpentine, a line with repeated gaps and a staggered line are all worth consideration.

RIGHT *These golden Irish yews (Taxus baccata 'Fastigiata Aureomarginata') are viewed through an archway of Carpinus betulus (hornbeam) hedging. The Irish yews, green or gold, are ideal to form compact columns, which are narrow in their youth but thicken up as they develop.*

FAR RIGHT *This picture of a border designed by Michael Balston illustrates how well topiary hedges work with grasses — an unusual but strikingly simple combination.*

Topiary can be traced back to the Greek civilization and, in one form or another, it has been popular in the West ever since. Mazes, labyrinths, colonnades, arbours, geometric and figurative shapes, unusual hedges, arches, gateways, and grand garden chessboards are just some of the features that can be made by clipping plants.

Today, topiary is more popular than ever. The bold structural dimensions that shaped evergreens can lend to a garden need not be reserved for large formal gardens; they also enhance small ones. Topiary can help define spaces in a garden in a bold, simple and extremely effective way. Shaped specimens can emphasize a particular feature, or define borders.

Simple shapes such as balls, pyramids or columns are easy to achieve and require relatively little maintenance. There is virtually unlimited scope for one's own creative inventions. The increased availability of so many different types of evergreen has also meant that one is no longer restricted to a few suitable plants.

TOPIARY HEDGES

Patience is needed for topiary hedges as they may take quite some time to develop, especially if you use slow-growing plants, such as yew or box. They are worth waiting for, however. They can be clipped into all sorts of patterns: a series of windows could be cut in them to create views into the next space; or the top edge could

be shaped into pyramids or balls. The line of the hedge need not be straight: it could be stepped in and out, made serpentine, or broken at regular intervals.

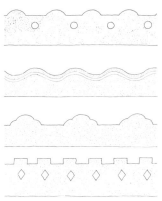

FIG. 15 *Topiary hedges*

Fast-growing conifers such as *Chamaecyparis lawsoniana* (lawson cypress) or *Thuja plicata* (thuja) will never achieve the tight-textured effect of clipped yew or box and they also require far more regular clipping. If you are impatient and want your hedge to thicken quickly, plant triple staggered rows at slightly closer stem centres (about 40cm [16in]) in both directions, and water copiously in dry periods, Yew responds especially well to this. Keep the surrounding area as weed-free as possible.

OFF-THE-PEG TOPIARY

Many growers produce a wide variety of geometrically shaped plants: balls in single, double or triple tiers, pyramids, cubes, obelisks, spirals. They also grow many different figurative shapes: cockerels, bears, birds in nests, swans, rabbits and ducks, to name but a few.

You can grow your own topiary by buying ready-made frames in all sort of shapes and sizes (see Suppliers' Guide) and training your plants around them. If you are more daring you can make the shape yourself. Sometimes the way a plant grows can suggest a particular shape. Try to buy plants that are fairly bushy, so you won't have too long to wait before they start taking on the desired form.

I enjoy propagating plants and over 10 years I have managed to grow some 90cm (3ft) cone-shaped box plants from cuttings. This may seem like a very long time, but they were planted in a rather dry and exposed area and although established in the ground as rooted cuttings rather than being kept in containers where growth is usually slower, they were not nurtured particularly attentively so it should be possible to improve on this timescale.

HERB TOPIARY

Herbs are usually quick-growing, and can be made into spectacular topiary shapes. Rosemary plants shaped as peacocks and cats were mentioned in Parkinson's *Paradisus in Sole* in 1629. Lavender is particularly quick-growing, and will form wonderful balls, though it will need frequent trimming during the growing season.

STANDARDS, MOPHEADS & BALLS

Standards and mopheads look wonderful in many gardens and they are very easy to create. I particularly like them arranged in bold groups, lines, squares or quincunxes (the name given to the pattern of five that you find on a dice). The large balls of foliage at eye level add a strong vertical dimension while framing the space that the group takes up. The height of plants trained like this can also be used to emphasize strong geometric patterns in the rest of the garden. Roses are traditionally made into standards but many other plants are suitable for the treatment, particularly evergreens which, of course, have the advantage of carrying the effect through the winter months.

Plants such as gooseberries, redcurrants, sweet bay and vines can be trained as standards and look especially fitting in a kitchen garden. If you are trying to grow a vine in cooler climates, keep it in a pot so that you can move it into the greenhouse over winter — although you should make sure it is unheated, vines require cool conditions if they are to generate flowers. A topdressing and a good feed in mid-spring is necessary. Gooseberries and redcurrants are usually grafted onto a more vigorous *Ribes* rootstock. Ungrafted, they would be rather short and not very sturdy. Roses are often grafted onto *Rosa rugosa*. The other plants that I have listed on page 109 are normally grown on their own roots.

Standards and mopheads are one of the simplest forms of topiary. To form a standard (Fig. 16) you have to grow a principal vertical stem, known as the leader,

RIGHT *The spherical perfection of these topiary balls contrasts satisfactorily with the wildness of the grass bank.*

FAR RIGHT *An example of some stunning planting at the Old Vicarage, East Ruston. The golden holly towers above the predominantly lower-level planting, while the box edging forms an elaborate frame that shows off the more informal, lower-level planting to its best.*

Pleaching

Pleaching is a traditional training technique which was very popular in medieval times. These 'hedges on stilts' can be invaluable for screening neighbouring eyesores. Although pleached trees are usually planted in double lines – usually in straight rows or gentle curves – they can be used in a single line to edge a small plot. Without being over-dominant they will still create much-valued privacy in built-up areas.

Although one usually sees pleached *Carpinus betulus* (hornbeam), *Fagus sylvatica* (beech) or *Tilia platyphyllos* (lime), most trees can be pleached – although something like a horse chestnut, for example, would be too vigorous and brittle. The pink hawthorn *Crataegus oxycantha* 'Paul's Scarlet' looks extremely attractive. The London plane (*Platanus × hispanica*) can be pleached but large nobbles tend to form at the ends of the shoots that are continually cut back, which looks unsightly.

CHOOSING THE TREE

When choosing the tree you must decide on the ultimate height you require. If you have a small garden, a less vigorous tree such as *Sorbus* (whitebeam) or *Carpinus betula* (hornbeam), which do not require so much pruning, is preferable. Once hornbeam is established, its neat leaves can be cut with hedge clippers in late spring.

You can buy ready-trained trees of up to 4m (13ft), with up to nine layers on them (see Suppliers' Guide), or you can transplant a 60–90cm (2–3ft) specimen, which will establish quickly. Between these two extremes, the usual choice would be a small standard with a girth of 6–8cm (2½–3in) and a height of 2.5–2.75m (8–9 ft).

RIGHT *These are* Crataegus oxycantha *'Coccinea Plena' (pink hawthorn) which have been pleached. Although hawthorns do indeed have thorns they don't develop until the second year, so training the young shoots is not quite as painful as it may seem.*

I find that the smaller plants establish more quickly and will often overtake plantings of more mature trees within four to five years. However, they need to be trained up a light cane in order to get a straight stem. Let the nursery know that you intend to pleach them, so they can help you select trees with branches that grow out predominantly in one plane.

Plant the trees along a straight line, about 1.5–2.5m (5–8ft) apart. If you are forming a double row, leave about 3m (10ft) between the rows, or more space depending on the design.

CHOOSING THE FRAMEWORK

If you are training your own trees you need to decide whether to erect a permanent framework or use bamboo canes to connect the adjacent shoots of trees at the same level. The former method is more expensive, but once done does make training a lot easier. The latter method is visually far less obtrusive but on very exposed sites it can prove to be rather fragile and may require regular refixing.

If you have bought ready-formed specimens, you only need to link the adjacent branches of one tree to another, using stout bamboo canes to ensure an even level. Secure the canes with a tree-tying tape called spindle bush, a thin plastic, tube-like material used by commercial nurseries (see Suppliers' Guide). The tape stretches as the tree grows and so does not cut into it. It is usually available in yellow or bright green – both unfortunate colours for camouflage. The yellow is more stretchy, but I use the green for pleaching as it holds the branches in place more firmly.

My garden is fairly exposed, so I trained my hornbeams along wire which is fixed to tall, black, tubular steel posts. These were drilled through the centre at the height of each level of branches so that the wires could be threaded through to provide a firm line for tying in the branches. The posts were driven about 60cm (2ft) into the ground. Timber posts, no thicker than 50 × 50cm (2 × 2ft), can be used instead as a temporary measure, to be removed once a densely woven screen has become established. Light timber horizontal battens, 50 × 25cm (2 × 1ft), fixed between the verticals would keep the whole structure rigid. The lowest horizontal is usually fixed at about 2m (5ft 6in), so that it is possible to walk underneath it. However, you may choose to position it lower if, for example, you want to screen something.

TOP RIGHT (FIG 18)

Year 1: A sturdy framework is necessary if the site is exposed. Otherwise use long, stout bamboo canes to take the place of the horizontal wires, attaching each end of the cane to the corresponding lateral from adjacent trees. Train the young trees up stout bamboo canes (not shown) to keep the trunk straight. Tie in the leader to the cane. Tie suitably positioned laterals firmly to the horizontal wires, remove all other laterals.

Year 2: When the leader reaches the top wire, bend it along the wire and tie it in, and bend a well positioned lateral from the adjacent trees along the top wire to meet it. Shorten any over long laterals back to a side shoot and shorten side shoots back to three buds to encourage growth. During the growing season remove all new growth except that growing sideways or that which can be trained to a wire and tied in. The aim is to fill in all the framework with growth.

Year 3: Cut back all new growth that grows beyond the framework to a bud, ideally keeping the top and bottom horizontal line straight. Tie in all well positioned shoots, and as the gaps between the tiers reduces, shoots can be tied in to their neighbouring shoots above and below. Wherever shoots are growing away from the vertical plane cut them back to a bud facing sideways. Generally the pruning is done in winter, though it is a good idea to neaten it up in early summer to keep it looking smart during the summer months.

RIGHT *This pleached lime walk leads the eye – and indeed the wandering visitor – along its length towards the gate at the end of the path.*

FAR RIGHT *As these pleached limes have their linear leaf canopy at eye level the eye is drawn towards the striking moon gateway. If you are an impatient gardener you can plant the young trees at closer centres, as close as 1.5m (5ft), to achieve a solid wall more quickly.*

TRAINING TREES FOR PLEACHING

Remove any lower side shoots, and any shoots that are not growing in the same plane as the support framework. Position the remaining laterals along the support, tying them in where necessary. Your aim is to fill the gaps and create a good dense screen or hedge on stilts. When you have established all the levels – the number depends on your requirements for height, but 3–9 is common – you can maintain it like a hedge.

VARIATIONS

There are variations in style of pleaching. The late David Hicks pleached hornbeams in a line with a solid hornbeam hedge at the lower level. Arches can be formed by planting two trees, bending them over an arch support and then pleaching the side branches horizontally.

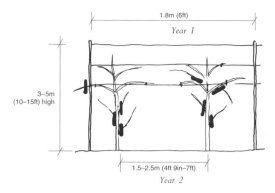
Year 1

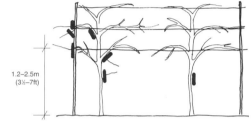
Year 2

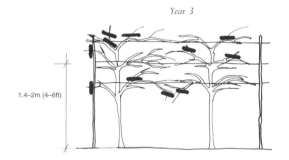
Year 3

FIG. 18 *Training trees for pleaching*

Colonnades, galleries & arbours

When you start training trees and shrubs you realize how versatile they are. Seeing the dramatic effect that completed colonnades, arbours or trained tree houses contribute to a garden is inspirational.

Using trained plants in different ways can be a very successful way of creating a highly individual space. This might be on a tiny scale: perhaps a short length of arcade to create an eye-catching end to a small town garden, or a weeping ash woven into a natural arbour. The time required can also be reduced by planting mature plants. To give some impact in the short term attractive metal or timber supporting structures can be used.

COLONNADES

Colonnades can be formed from trees trained into columns – usually *Taxus baccata* (yew), *Fagus sylvatica* (beech), or *Carpinus betulus* (hornbeam) – which are planted in a line often running parallel to a hedge or wall. Very often a timber horizontal connects the top of the column with the hedge, forming a partial overhead screen (Fig. 19). The idea is to achieve the effect of a cloister with the columns enclosing a central space, but even a single line can be most effective.

Forming a Colonnade

In order to make the trees resemble columns, they should be clipped to follow the shape of a column, that is, have a shaped base, a vertical shaft and a 'capital' at the top. They will need posts to guide them while they grow. A plinth, in the form of a low clipped hedge, can be grown along the base in a straight line between the columns.

The height of the columns should be between 2.4m and 3m (7ft 8in and 10ft) so that they align with any surrounding architecture. A 'beam' of branches is trained horizontally by attaching stout canes or battens to the vertical posts supporting the trees.

Above this level the plant which forms the vertical column may have its trunk exposed for about 10cm (4in) and then a finial such as a ball is formed to terminate the column. The diameter of the column should be narrow, about 30–60cm (1–2ft), so as to resemble stone columns.

Using a Framework

Incorporating a non-organic material such as metal to form an attractive framework up which the plants grow

FIG. 19 *Colonnade*

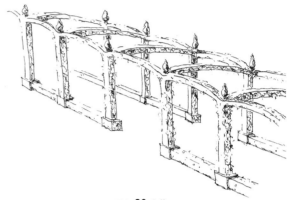

FIG. 20 *Gallery*

can make the colonnade look terrific. You get a feel of the colonnade well before the plants have reached maturity and the metal column which surrounds the plant provides an edge to cut to (see Suppliers' Guide).

GALLERIES

These 'green galleries' are formed from two parallel rows of plants clipped in a columnar fashion and then arched at the top so they meet both the plants in the same row and their opposite number in the parallel row. A skeleton structure, made from either metal or wood, is required to get the regular arch shape. It does take quite a time to achieve the arches, but a decorative framework provides a very acceptable stand-in for the early years.

The treatment of the columns is variable: they could imitate traditional columns like those used in colonnades (see above) or perhaps have exposed trunks free of green foliage for part of the way. Alternatively, exposed trunks and finials could be formed above the arches, or timber or metal finials could be substituted so that the routine clipping was more straightforward and at a slightly lower level.

Decorative fruit

An area for growing vegetables and fruit is, for me, a favourite part of any garden. Even an unkempt orchard has a great deal of charm when strewn with fallen apples or blossom and tall clumps of foxgloves and long grasses simply embellish the scene.

ORCHARDS

Orchards can be highly decorative. John Stefanidis has emphasized the trunks of the trees with low-growing domes of foliage in his orchard at Cock Crow Farm in Southern England. Plump cushions of *Hebe rakiensis* grow around the base of apple trees, which are planted on a grid. The trees are heavily pruned each year to allow enough light for the hebes. Hebes grow fast and tend to get gappy when older, so he replaces them every six years or so to keep a well-covered look. A similar effect was achieved in an orchard in the south of France, using box instead of hebe. Box needs an annual clip in early summer and takes longer to shape, but it does not need replacing every six years or so and will tolerate shade.

Another way to add ornamental value to your orchard is to train the trees in different forms. Fruit trees have been grafted, pruned and trained into diverse shapes for thousands of years by skilled Europeans, particularly French gardeners, and will take almost any form.

CHOOSING THE TREES

When you choose your plant material, go for high-quality one-year-old maidens with side shoots (feathers). These plants receive less of a shock when transplanted than larger trees. They also establish quickly, allowing their subsequent vigorous growth to speed up the training.

Container-grown larger trees suffer a shock on planting out as they have often been potted up quite recently

prior to being sold. Alternative problems occur if the containers have been around for too long – the root system becomes compacted within the compost and after planting out never branches out into the soil to establish a good root hold. Choose plants grafted onto a dwarfing rootstock, such as M9 and M26 for apples, and Quince C and A for pears. For the larger formations such as fruit arches, MM106 would be more suitable. The growers are usually able to guide you as to the most suitable rootstock for the effect you want to achieve.

SUMMER PRUNING

There are practical advantages to elaborately trained fruit. It is economical in terms of space and most of the pruning can be done in late summer. This involves the shortening of the side shoots produced from the permanent branches. It is extremely easy to do but the timing is critical. If it is done too early the dormant buds will grow in autumn. Wait until the shoots are about as thick as a pencil and are hard at the base. Ideally, the terminal bud will be fat, indicating that growth has finished for that year. The shoots growing from a main branch should be cut back to approximately 7.5cm (3in) or three leaves above the basal cluster. Any shoots formed from a spur should be pruned back to 2.5cm (1in) or one leaf above the basal cluster.

A permanent framework makes pruning the fruit tree simpler and the training much more straightforward. Where a permanent framework is needed, metal has the advantage of being visually far lighter than wood, although it can be a little more expensive. Most blacksmiths enjoy the challenge of producing something a little out of the ordinary and can advise on the necessary size and type of metal to use.

ABOVE *This is a winged pyramid which is fairly complicated to form. At about 30cm (1ft) from the ground six shoots are trained out from the trunk and then taken upwards on the pyramid frame. This is repeated at 60cm (2ft) intervals up the trunk. Notice the straight sides to the pyramid.*

RIGHT *This apple tree has been trained as a table top. To achieve this, eight shoots were trained to radiate out from the centre, as spokes do from a wheel. When these shoots reached the desired diameter, they were trained round a metal framework into a circle and then grafted together.*

BELOW *Here is a fantastic and productive green arch grown from apple trees. Do not be daunted by the time it would take to form this, as vertical shoots do grow fast. You will need to sacrifice fruit in the first few years to channel the energy into forming the basic shape.*

Willow

The flexible nature of willow has been exploited for many, many years. As well as its horticultural uses, willow also gives us the origins of aspirin (acetylsalicyclic acid), furniture wickerwork, paper pulp and charcoal. It is currently being cultivated for burning as a renewable energy source.

Willow's popularity for garden use is no doubt due to its rapid establishment and growth, producing almost instant effects. It can form living fences and arches, huts, tunnels, sculptures and arbours. It is also useful for stabilizing steep banks, particularly by streams. For this it can be woven into a growing hedge bank *in situ* (see page 57).

Willows will establish well even when they are grown in poor, dry soil conditions. For this reason willow is regularly used in reclamation projects in coal spoil and quarry slopes. It is effective because its root action and abundant leaf litter improve the physical structure and the nutrient content of really poor soils, and it also provides shelter and a more hospitable environment for other plants.

Willows will survive in highly compacted soils as well as fast-draining ones, though they excel in moist conditions. In areas where there is a high level of atmospheric pollution or very compacted soil, *Salix viminalis* 'Bowles hybrid', *S. daphnioides* 'Continental Purple' or *S.d.* 'Oxford Violet' are recommended by Steve Pickup, who specializes in willows, supplying many varieties in plant, cutting, rod or bundle form (see Suppliers' Guide).

WILLOW RETAINING WALLS

Retaining walls can be an expensive, as well as intrusive, element in a natural area of garden. An alternative is to use growing willow. To form a retaining wall of willow, you may initially need to use a purpose-made netting (see Suppliers' Guide) pinned to the bank to stabilize it. During the dormant season, take rods of *Salix*

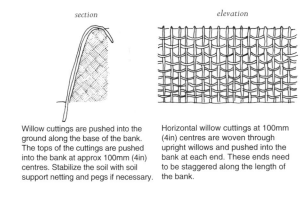

section   elevation

Willow cuttings are pushed into the ground along the base of the bank. The tops of the cuttings are pushed into the bank at approx 100mm (4in) centres. Stabilize the soil with soil support netting and pegs if necessary.

Horizontal willow cuttings at 100mm (4in) centres are woven through upright willows and pushed into the bank at each end. These ends need to be staggered along the length of the bank.

FIG 21 *Willow retaining wall*

*viminalis (*willow) that are the height of the bank, plus a further length of about 30cm (1ft) to firm into the soil top and bottom. Push them into the ground in a row at the bottom of the bank and then at the top.

The planting centres of the cuttings can vary between 15 and 30cm (6in and 1ft), depending on the appearance

RIGHT *A lovely, informal boundary to this country garden is formed from a growing woven willow fence planted in a serpentine shape. It forms an effective solid barrier at the base and a see-through barrier at the top. It was designed and constructed by Ewan McEwan.*

FAR RIGHT *This exciting tree tunnel and bridge was designed and made by Clare Wilks from hazel, ash and willow.*

you are seeking. The thickness of the cuttings will vary, but the sturdy two-year-old cuttings, which may be 25mm (1in) in diameter, are the largest that are recommended for use unless you have a very high water table. These are obtainable up to about 2.8m (15ft) long.

Once the verticals are in place, weave the horizontals in and out of the verticals, fixing the two ends into the bank before and after weaving each rod. These can be smaller, whippier sections of willow. You can make the weaving as tight or widely spaced as you like, but the aim will be to hide the soil.

Maintenance is as for most living willow structures and is quite demanding. Early each spring you trim back the previous season's growth. In late spring you can start weaving in the new growths. Push some of these into the soil to fill out barer patches. After the third year, when most of the structure is fairly thickly woven, you then need to cut it back hard in early spring, and as necessary during the growing season.

Competition from weeds hampers establishment, so make sure your soil is pretty weed-free before you start (a fallow period for a month or so in good growing conditions is ideal).

WALLS

Willow walls can also be formed to act as both noise and visual barriers (as can willow hedge banks, see Fig 6, page 57). They are usually constructed by specialists (see Suppliers' Guide). There are different techniques but they all basically involve clay- and rubble-filled battered bunds about 5m (16ft) wide and 2–3m (6–9ft) high, built up in layers which are stabilized with a mesh and have a 15cm (6in) layer of topsoil on the outside. The willow cuttings are then pushed into the bund between the layers where a 10cm (4in) additional topsoil layer has also been positioned.

WILLOW ARBOURS

On a more domestic scale, the living willow arbour shown in Fig. 22 was designed by Clare Wilks (see Suppliers' Guide) for the Herbalists' Garden which I designed for Wyevale Garden Centres for Chelsea 1998. It was constructed during early spring, when the material is at its prime, for exhibiting three months later. It is a good example of the diversity of willow: dense weaving for the seat, the splendid, tapering, closely woven, Gothic type arch and finally the wispy latticework.

RIGHT *This growing willow arch with seating alcoves was designed and made by Clare Wilks out of living and dried willow.*

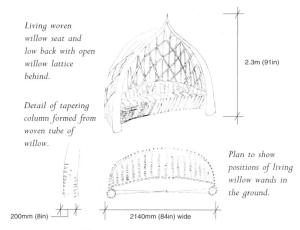

Living woven willow seat and low back with open willow lattice behind.

Detail of tapering column formed from woven tube of willow.

2.3m (91in)

Plan to show positions of living willow wands in the ground.

200mm (8in)

2140mm (84in) wide

FIG 22 *Willow arbour (see photograph on page 51)*

water
& lighting

 **W**ATER IS COMPELLING IN THE GARDEN AND ASTONISHINGLY VERSATILE IN THE RANGE OF MOODS IT CAN CREATE, FROM THE CALM SERENITY EVOKED BY DEEP LIMPID POOLS TO THE THRILL OF FAST-MOVING FOUNTAIN JETS. WATER HAS ALWAYS BEEN PARTICULARLY PRIZED AND IMAGINATIVELY USED IN HOT, DRY CLIMATES, WHERE COOL SHADE, LUSH PLANTINGS AND SPARKLING WATER GLITTERING IN THE SUN COMBINE TO CREATE HIGHLY DESIRABLE SPACES. HOWEVER, EVEN IN COOL MARITIME CLIMATES WHERE WATER IS MORE AVAILABLE AND LESS PRECIOUS, THE APPEAL OF PONDWEED AND STREAMS, RUNNING WATER AND MOSSY PEBBLES HAS A VERY SPECIAL CHARM. PERHAPS BECAUSE DWELLING PLACES HAVE HISTORICALLY BEEN SITED AS CLOSE TO WATER AS POSSIBLE, A GARDEN SEEMS STRANGELY INCOMPLETE WITHOUT IT.

Still water

BELOW *This recently constructed bassin in the grounds of a French farmhouse is very simple but most effective. The high water level together with the detailing of the stonework to the pier which provides the inlet are key contributors to its success. Designed by the French architect, Jean-Louis Germain.*

Still water features are the simplest to design and the easiest to make work. Whether formal or informal, use the style and mood of the rest of your garden — and indeed house — to set the style for the pool. One of my favourite examples of a still pool is in the garden of a small château set in a beautiful lush valley in France (see below). The design is based on the local stone water storage tanks known as *bassins* which are common throughout the south of France. Although the purpose of the original *bassins* was primarily functional — as a water source for the house and garden — this modern version, a sunken pool of simple shape with a well-made stone coping and small obelisk at one end, was built purely for aesthetic reasons. Its success lies in its simplicity and the wholly appropriate way that it blends into its magical setting, echoing an age-old architectural feature.

RAISED POOLS

If you do not have a particularly distinctive setting that calls out for a special approach, you may wish to incorporate more interest into the pool itself. One way to achieve this is to raise the pool to accentuate its shape. The raised sides could be made of brick, stone, granite or rendered blockwork. Alternatively, you could plant a dwarf hedge immediately around the edge, clipped to form gentle scalloped curves with gaps in between to form 'sitting bays'. Raised sides make ideal seating areas, but the detailing must be good, as they come under close scrutiny. If you are using a butyl liner, black is the best colour to choose. Have a large overhang on the coping — a minimum of 50mm (2in) — and ideally clad the sides to a depth of 15cm (6in) below the coping with stone or brick to hide the liner.

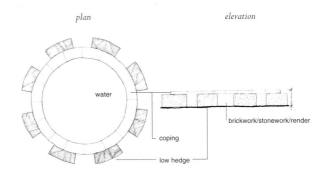

plan   elevation

water

brickwork/stonework/render

coping

low hedge

FIG 23 *Small hedges surrounding raised pools are an interesting detail. The drawback is that the planting frustrates the common desire to* *sit on the edge of the pool. One way to solve this is to interrupt the hedging with gaps where people can gain access to the water.*

RIGHT *In this pool designed by Michael Balston, the clipped green box hedges around the raised pool are a superb addition, anchoring the formal pool to the pattern work of the surrounding planting.*

FAR RIGHT *The sides of this raised pool have been softened by the copious planting that surrounds them. The plants are contained within bold pots on the piers and within the centre-piece. The four square piers are made of tiles and stand slightly proud of the circular coping, breaking up the line. It is at the Old Vicarage, East Ruston.*

ADDING DETAIL

In a clear, sparkling, formal pool the base is highly visible so it responds well to decorating in some way. You could form eye-catching spirals with ammonites, intricate patterns with mosaic tiles, beautiful designs with pebble paving set in mortar, or simply throw in loose glittering shapes of gold or silver glass. I once designed a shell garden where I used shellwork to decorate the entrance arches and the seats and loose shells as mulching for the plants. I rendered the raised sides of the pool, and then set thousands of shells in the render. More usually, clear formal pools may have loose pebbles covering the base, but many paving materials such as stone slabs, bricks (of special quality), slate laid in patterns or a mix of materials are excellent finishes to lay over the waterproof liner.

ABOVE *The unusual effect created here is made by paving flowing into the pool in giant ripples formed from resin-bonded crushed mauve glass to give a cohesive, flowing effect. It was designed by Bonita Bulaitis.*

FAR RIGHT (ABOVE) *The stone edging on this pool, which I designed, is blue lias, which was then continued down the sides with no overhang to form a coursed stone finish. The butyl liner was completely hidden as the base of the pool was formed from York slabs cut in a circular pattern. The dragon was carved by English Limestone Products (see Suppliers' Guide).*

RIGHT *A narrow band of metal, preferably stainless steel painted black if preferred, gives a sharp edge to a pool. This can be fitted on top of the flexible liner. Designed by Christopher Bradley-Hole.*

FAR RIGHT *The circular pool of water with the linear clump of aquatic grasses is full of intricate detail. It is edged with a circle of wild flowers and the beautifully decorated container has a silver-grey finish incorporating sparkling motifs. The tiny fountain is also decorated.*

Moving water

The noise of water, whether it is running, trickling, spurting, or gently plopping, is appealing in its own right, but it is also useful for distracting your ear from unwanted background noise. Another positive asset is the ambience which it creates. This is partly caused by the negative ions which are discharged into the air by running water and lead to feelings of happiness and contentment. Positive ions, which have the reverse effect, are found in dry, desert conditions. The range of emotions running water can evoke ranges from the sense of exhilaration generated by high-reaching jets to the calm relaxation caused by a gentle trickle.

FOUNTAINS

Moving water is increasingly feasible in private gardens as technology becomes more efficient and pumps and fountains can do more and more spectacular things. The simplest moving-water feature is a fountain and the options are almost infinite. Your choice will really be a matter of personal preference – there are all manner of

pool centrepieces from stone dragons snorting water to stone bowls ever refilling and trickling over. Projecting a more high-tech feel are the nozzle and jet fittings which can spray jets in whichever pattern you choose. Narrow columns of water ranging from 75cm to 6m (2ft 5in to 19ft 8in) in height and ejected from single nozzles can look particularly effective when used in straight or curved sequences to fit the shape of the pool. Alternatively, you can opt for neat parasols, pirouettes, fountain crowns, water bells, solid sheets, foam effects, vertical cascades, geysers and water spheres. The choice is endless (see Suppliers' Guide).

If it is windy, any fountain in an exposed situation will gust about and particularly so if the water shoots up high. The main drawback is that you will have to top up the water level regularly to maintain the level, but you will also risk getting soaked when you pass by. As a rule of thumb you should restrict the height of the jet to the distance from the nozzle to the edge of the pool – although this is by no means failsafe.

RIGHT *This pool with its simple fountain jet is the midway point along the length of a cascade flanked by tall yew hedges in a Lincolnshire garden. The cascade is surrounded by predominantly moisture-loving plants to add to the naturalistic feel. As the soil is naturally very free draining I designed these planting beds to have a polythene liner (with a few drainage holes) sunk to a depth of 600mm (2ft) to increase the moisture retention of the soil.*

ORNAMENTAL FOUNTAIN CENTREPIECE

If you decide to set a fountain centrepiece at the heart of your water feature, you could search through architectural reclamation yards and perhaps be lucky enough to find an antique, or else purchase a reproduction one, which will usually be made from lead or reconstituted

TOP RIGHT *Irregular layers contain this small fountain jet ideally suited to a courtyard garden and enhanced by lush planting. It was designed by Jean Melville-Clarke.*

TOP FAR RIGHT *This water feature consists of a stainless steel sheet which has two holes in the top allowing water to flow continually over the shimmering metal sheet. It creates a mesmerizing effect as the clear water makes fascinating patterns over the shiny surface.*

BELOW RIGHT *The more traditional approach of this wall fountain designed by Anthony Noel has been well put together. The lion's mask spurts water onto a stone trough overflowing with pebbles. The surrounding planting forms a good contrast to the harder lines of the wall and trough.*

BELOW FAR RIGHT *This galvanized iron and copper water fountain forms a focal point in a small London garden. It is about 3m (10ft) high and helps to break up a tall, dominant brick wall. It was designed and built by Ralph Levy.*

stone. Alternatively, you could consider commissioning one. There are many craftsmen who work in stone, concrete, bronze, lead, glass, stainless steel, perspex, granite and wood, and who would relish the opportunity to create something a bit different. It is not unusual for custom-made items to work out cheaper than their mass-produced equivalents.

Illusions with water

MAKING A GOLDEN BALL FOUNTAIN

The perpetually moving golden ball designed by Robin Williams is not only strangely hypnotic but also introduces a note of humour into a garden. It is a simple, clever concept which could be adapted in a number of ways. As you can see from the photograph, four jets on each corner appear to be holding up and balancing a golden ball, which is in fact tied with nylon string to the base of a cylindrical glass tube. This tube is fixed to a horizontal perspex board with a hole cut in its base and hidden by a layer of shiny coal. Wash the coal first otherwise the coal dust will stain. The water is forced up the tube through the hole and makes the ball (which is plastic painted gold) bob up and down. The overflow of water from both the four jets and from the centre help to conceal the perspex tube.

RIGHT AND BELOW *A striking effect is created by this golden ball which appears to be bobbing on top of the fountain. As can be seen from the illustration, it is a clever illusion and not too tricky to make.*

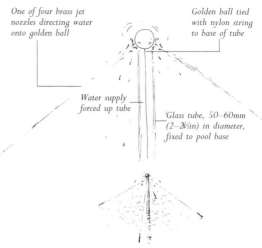

One of four brass jet nozzles directing water onto golden ball

Golden ball tied with nylon string to base of tube

Water supply forced up tube

Glass tube, 50–60mm (2–2¼in) in diameter, fixed to pool base

FIG 24 *Golden ball fountain*

Flowing water

Water features designed to imitate nature, such as cascades, streams and waterfalls, require careful thought, design and detailing if they are to look convincing. All the artificial elements must be hidden, and meanders and bends must be carefully scaled to look natural.

RILLS

A simple rill is a delightful addition to a garden. These understated, small channels of water, which can be made to flow into a pool, fit very easily into most surroundings. They can travel across formal paved areas, meander around a lawn, or wind through informal planting. Birds and wildlife are attracted to the shallow water.

As rills are generally structural with no plants growing in them, it is best not to form them from butyl liner alone, which tends to be too visible unless you use a coping with a generous overhang. Rills are frequently made of concrete (perhaps coloured, textured or with an exposed aggregate finish), brick or stone over the liner. Or you could have a rill made as a simple vertical-sided channel running with close-mown grass growing virtually to the edge of the water, so underplaying the 'hard paving' effect. To achieve this you need to fix a thin, upright edge of hardwood timber or black steel over the concrete and butyl construction. The grass edge will need constant trimming as the mower cannot run over it. These rills look good, but require regular maintenance.

CASCADES

There is a famous cascade at Chatsworth, Derbyshire, England where the water tumbles down into pools at different levels in a very spectacular fashion. Scaled-down versions for the domestic garden capture the flavour equally well. One approach is to have water spilling out over a weir edge so that it tumbles some distance from the vertical face. In order to make the water project outwards you can fix small, thin, stainless

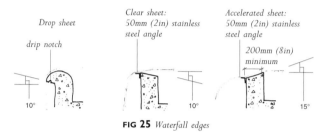

FIG 25 *Waterfall edges*

steel plates which are barely noticeable to the top of the weir. They can be straight for a flat sheet of water or wavy-edged so that the water falls in a pattern. Glass, stone tiles and slate can be also be used to achieve a similar effect.

RIGHT (FIG. 25) *Three profiles for a waterfall edge are illustrated here. The profile affects the water as it spills over. The one on the left causes the water to form a 'drop sheet'. The middle one forms a 'clear sheet' of water and employs a 50mm (2in) stainless steel right angle which is fixed to the concrete upstand. The one on the right also employs the stainless steel right angle as above, thrown over in an 'accelerated sheet'.*

ABOVE RIGHT *Here the water cascades over an artificial fibreglass rock into a large pool. The rock was made large enough to allow a path to travel under the rushing water. It formed part of the tropical garden I designed for Wyevale Garden Centres at Chelsea Flower Show in 1996.*

BELOW RIGHT *Here stepping stones through the shallows form an exciting route for the intrepid. Hardwood is obviously preferable; elm is ideal as it hardens in water and lasts hundreds of years. Position the steps on the pool base (usually a liner) by providing concrete haunching. It is also necessary to provide a concrete or firm platform directly under the liner where the stepping stone or log will be positioned to transfer the load.*

BELOW FAR RIGHT *Christine Pritchard designed this bridge and waterfall for Wyevale Garden Centres for their Cotswold Garden. The cascade is formed from dry-stone walling, as is the bridge.*

SLOW-MOVING WATER

If you require a naturalistic effect from your slow-moving water, you may well want to think carefully about planting on the banks. If you want the feature to look like a stream that would fit into the local landscape, use native plants such as ivies, rushes and ferns. Exotic plants would work if you want more impact and are less concerned with imitating nature. The problem is usually to provide moisture-retentive soil around an artificially formed water feature. To overcome this, make sure that the butyl liner extends well back under the surrounding banks which are then re-formed with the soil. Alternatively you can create separate bog gardens either side of the water channel using a polythene liner with drainage holes buried well below the surface.

TOP RIGHT *This artificial stream was designed by Sarah Raven. The base of the channel is broken up by irregular, weathered old stones and the adjacent planting, which is part native, part exotic, encroaches over the sides, breaking them up to create a convincing stretch of moving water.*

RIGHT *This stretch of moving water has a shallow base of irregular stone flags which conceal the liner below. The adjacent strips of planting are formed in linear artificial bog gardens. Other architectural plants which prefer drier conditions, such as the purple cordylines (Cordyline australis purpurea) are planted in large pots.*

Bridges, boardwalks, platforms

Water seems to have almost magnetic powers, drawing all ages to get as close to it as possible. A timber pier, simple stepping stones or wide steps leading down to the water's edge all provide interesting access points, while boardwalks and bridges get you close to the water by elevating you over it.

STEPPING STONES

Stepping stones are simple structures that can be made from heavy hardwood logs, brick or stone piers topped with a slab, or even, if you can get them, large flat-topped rocks. Whatever you use needs to be anchored firmly to the well-protected butyl liner or pool base by set lumps of concrete. There must be a firm, well blinded hardcore base below the liner too. Stepping stones need not be in a single line; they can form strong visual statements when arranged in bold groupings, and are then also easier to use for the faint-hearted.

If the span of water you want to cross is narrow, a simple plank of wood – or long length of stone or concrete – can be supported entirely or partially from the banks. If timber is being used in a position that water reaches it must be a hardwood of durable quality. Timber gets slimy and slippery when it rains, so it is better either to keep it for very short stretches or else design it with a generous width and possibly a handrail. Chicken wire can be fixed over timber to aid gripping but it is a bit of an eyesore, or the timber can be textured wth grooves.

BOARDWALKS

Boardwalks skirting around the edge of the water are an ideal way to conceal butyl liner and provide safe access to the water's edge and an attractive path virtually at water level. If you have the space you can widen them to form an expansive seating area practically surrounded by water and luxuriant foliage, ideal for observing wildlife at close quarters.

RIGHT *This boardwalk skirts round a pool which, apart from providing a boardwalk with a difference, also serves to hide the sometimes difficult junction between the pool edge and the side. The butyl liner surfaces under the decking. The planks were whitewashed, as were the support posts. Large Gunnera manicata invades the decking, breaking up the gently curved edge.*

BELOW *These beautifully positioned concrete stepping stones give a modern, clean look to an otherwise very natural-looking stretch of water. The generous proportions and tiny gaps allow you to cross with no fears.*

BRIDGES

While low-level decking, boardwalks and paths seem to merge effortlessly with water features, bridges can do just the opposite, being by their very nature prominent. Humpback bridges, bridges with integrated arches, or stylish brightly coloured red, white, blue or bright green bridges immediately grab your attention.

Clare Wilks' spectacular Gothic-shaped bridge is woven together from young pliable stems of indigenous woods. The main structure is made from oak while the arched gallery above is made from willow (see page 114). Synthetic rope has been threaded through logs to make the bridge. It looks a little precarious but any feelings of instability are lessened by the secure nature of the top.

SAFE WATER FOR CHILDREN

Water is a particular attraction to children, not least because of the wildlife that always takes up residence. Unfortunately water represents a hazard to small children even if it is only a few centimetres deep, but rather than exclude it altogether, it is possible to design it so that it is safer.

The simplest option is to have something small, such as a bubble fountain or a wall fountain. A tiny shallow

rill is ideal for sailing boats, pooh sticks (provided you can position a makeshift bridge over it) and other types of games. A very shallow stream trickling over gravels, boulders and pebbles, with a depth of no more than 50mm (2in), will be a continual source of fascination to children and wildlife, and will not be too great a hazard.

If there are small children, I would keep any water depth below 50mm (2in) either by filling up the base of any pool or pond with sand and gravel to temporarily reduce its depth, or by allowing the water to drain out when supervision is not possible, thereby removing the hazard altogether. Alternatively, you can surround the pool with an attractive child-proof picket fence.

Underwater Grids

When my children were small, I designed an underwater grid which rested on parallel steel bars spanning the width of the pool, the grid was 50mm (2in) below the water level. The ends of the 3mm (⅛in) bars were welded onto flat metal brackets hooked over the coping at either end. Water lilies and other aquatic plants grew up through the grid, making it virtually invisible, and black non-toxic paint helped conceal it still further. Only the black metal brackets over the coping remained conspicuous, but you could choose to position them so they go under the copings. The disadvantage of doing this is that they are then fixed permanently, so you must position the grid with wire ties in order to have easy access for thinning out water plants and carrying out other general maintenance.

You can have an underwater grid even in a soft-edged, unevenly shaped pool by bolting the straps into metal post supports driven into the ground and filling the edges of informal curves with thick planting and pebbles.

RIGHT *A pendulous willow partially obscures a small timber humpback bridge which crosses a deep ravine. The handrail is supported by widely spaced uprights to prevent the structure looking too heavy.*

BELOW *This timber bridge crosses a drainable puddling pool which is surfaced with pebbles set in mortar, covering a butyl liner. I designed it as part of my first garden for the Chelsea Flower Show in 1994, which was A Garden for Children.*

Lighting

Lighting should enhance the best elements of your garden, picking out special features and highlighting the most attractive areas. If you are not happy with certain things, do not draw attention to them by lighting them. Unfortunately, there are many schemes which, instead of making the garden look special, go overboard by flooding everything with light, including conspicuous fittings, so that what should be a private space looks more like the forecourt of a hotel. The secret to remember is that darkness is as important as light. It is shades of darkness, and the different patterns of shadows, that create a magical atmosphere. When it is managed well, you should not even be aware that a lighting system exists. The most obvious tip is to remember to hide the light sources. In the same way that light in the theatre plays a large part in creating atmosphere, but does not reveal its sources, so garden lighting should seem to magically appear from nowhere.

DRAMATIC UPLIGHTING

Uplighters, when fully recessed into the ground, are easy to hide and create a dramatic highlighting effect. Ideally positioned at the base of trees, shrubs or a fine stone archway, they emphasize the feature in a more vivid way than daylight. It is possible to site them in hard surfaces and some will tolerate being driven over, but it is more difficult to conceal them than when they are put among planting or long grass. Some will light an area 20 degrees off the vertical.

BELOW *This plant box has been brought to life by some subtle hidden uplighters which throw the light onto the reflective surface behind the planting. It was designed by George Carter.*

RIGHT *This wall and surrounding planting is dramatically lit from below, giving the planting a translucent look. The scheme was designed by Sonny Garcia.*

RIGHT *Two spotlights which have a covering of glass chippings uplight a pathway by shining the light through the chippings, creating subtle definition to the path's edge. The lighting was designed by Garden and Security Lighting (see Suppliers' Guide).*

MAKING SHADOWS

Downlighting sends down beams of light from up high to graze vertical structures and create pools of light below them. The patterns of the shadows are the exciting part of this system. The fittings can be difficult to hide, although trees or a climber-clad pergola are ideal for concealing them. Use in moderation otherwise the effect will lose its charm. Uplighters also create shadows, although for this effect the fittings must be hidden at ground level.

Uplighters and downlighters can also be used to back light and wall wash, creating shadowy intimate effects. Position the uplighters or downlighters on a wall behind some trees or large shrubs so the plants are thrown in shadow, which accentuates their form as well as adding to the atmosphere.

SPOTLIGHTING

Spotlighting is a narrow beam of light which will pick out a particularly prized feature, giving it the 'main part' on the garden's stage. It must be placed some distance away from the object you want to pick out and works best if handled subtly, only illuminating part of the object and always concealing the source. For instance, if you are lighting a statue, a single beam directed straight would look rather obvious; lighting both sides would be too much; but a spotlight from the side would create a dramatic effect.

SOFT, ROMANTIC LIGHTING

Moonlight has a romantic, magical effect that appeals to most people and it is possible to create it artificially. Moonlighting fittings should be positioned high up in a

ABOVE LEFT *An oriental lantern emits a low level of soft lighting over the water and the planting.*

ABOVE CENTRE *Water comes into its own when it is lit up. Here a raised pool is partially covered with stepping stones which are lit by the light source in the water, emphasizing the strong diamond pattern which is carried through the space.*

ABOVE RIGHT *These obelisks designed by George Carter highlight an entrance. The doorway itself also emits a warming glow, providing a welcoming feel to the visitor.*

RIGHT *These illustrations show the effects created by different lighting fixtures.*

Spotlighting

Low-level wash lighting

Backlighting

mature tree, to prevent the light from glaring, and allowed to wash gently over lawns, beds and paved areas. It should create dappled shadows like those that occur when there is a full moon and clear skies.

WATER AND LIGHTING

Water and lighting work magically together. Mirror lighting, used in conjunction with pools or large expanses of water, is an alternative to underwater lighting. Its aim is to illuminate certain far objects, such as trees, urns or sculptures, which are then reflected in the water. It is a most effective and subtle lighting scheme.

LIGHTING THE WAY

Glare-free lighting for paving, steps and terraces makes it safe and enjoyable to use the garden after dark. Low-

level wash lighting is the name given to fittings which are about 200–600mm (8in–2ft) high and usually hidden in planting areas. The fittings may be traditional lantern types or simple lights on metal posts, and they may have spikes which allow one to move them around. Although popular because of their valuable functionality, the fittings can be conspicuous and so add little to the garden's atmosphere.

COMBINATION OF TECHNIQUES

It is not necessary to restrict yourself to one method of lighting for a particular area. For example, you could light a covered seat or an arbour framework with uplighters from below, while concealed downlighters pick out pots and planting around the seat. Two lighting circuits will allow you more sophisticated permutations.

LOW-KEY LIGHTING

There are simple, low-key lighting alternatives which are perfect for many gardens. Temporary options such as lanterns, candles, flares, nightlights and storm lanterns are inexpensive, romantic and fun. They can be hung or positioned in accessible areas, and require no disruption of carefully nurtured plant beds or pools. They can never give too much glare, so they are an ideal choice if you are worried about getting a brash effect. To supplement their rather piecemeal nature, you could try to find antique lanterns. They would be a visual asset even when unlit as well as making your nightime garden look very special.

Moonlighting

Mirror lighting

Uplighting

salvage

**T**HE USE OF SALVAGED
ITEMS IN PRIVATE GARDENS
IS GAINING MOMENTUM.
SEARCHING FOR QUIRKY
AND UNUSUAL MATERIALS
CAN BECOME AN ABSORBING OCCUPA-
TION AS WELL AS AN ECOLOGICALLY
SOUND ONE AND USING SALVAGED BITS
AND PIECES ENABLES YOU TO CREATE A
UNIQUE DESIGN. IT TAKES A CERTAIN
AMOUNT OF SKILL, PRACTISE AND IMAGI-
NATION TO IDENTIFY THE POTENTIAL OF
ODD SALVAGE ITEMS THAT ARE WORTH
DISPLAYING. PIECES OF STRANGELY
CARVED STONE – PERHAPS PART OF A
MOULDED PLINTH, FOR EXAMPLE –
COULD BE INSTANTLY TRANSFORMED
INTO AN UNUSUAL STONE BENCH BY
PUTTING A STONE SLAB ACROSS THE TOP.
ALTERNATIVELY, THE REMAINS OF A
CARVED STONE ARCH COULD BE INCOR-
PORATED INTO A RENDERED WALL TO
FRAME A VIEW.

Practicalities

It helps to have an eye for salvage, but you will also need to use common sense in your forages. For example, if you are lucky enough to come across some carved stone columns and want to use them to frame an outdoor entrance, make sure that the stone is suitable for external situations. Some stones are soft, and will quickly erode in freezing and wet weather. Stone that has been kept indoors for long periods will have become very dry, and once positioned outside it will absorb water very quickly. If the weather turns cold this water may freeze and shatter the stone. This advice applies even to York stone flags.

Sealing the stone to prevent water absorption could provide a solution. However, some sealants colour stonework, even though they are labelled 'clear', so test a small area first and leave it for a few weeks to check there is no colour change.

Salvaged bricks can be problematic. External bricks used for paving and wall copings are subjected to very damp conditions and extreme temperature variations, but there is no way of knowing whether the bricks you have chosen will be suitable for this outdoor use. Generally a dark, well-fired brick, as opposed to a pale one, will be more frost-resistant, although London stocks, which have mixed yellow tones, are usually adequate. However, be prepared to accept that if you use salvage bricks most probably a few will 'blow' and start to disintegrate when the winter frosts get to them. Hopefully that will be the limit of the damage.

You also need to take care when choosing stone flags. Often these are reclaimed from mills where they were in contact with oil, tar or other chemicals. Because of their porous nature, little trace of this will be visible until they are laid outside in the garden and exposed to sunlight, when they will suddenly turn black. The only way to overcome this problem is to try to find out where the flags came from. Railway sleepers may also have been contaminated with oil and tar, which will start oozing out in warm conditions, so make sure you select clean ones.

RIGHT *This stunning garden building is a great find. It was an old plant room forming part of a much larger building and has now been converted into a dovecote occupying a key position beside a large lake. The blue/grey finish works well against both the water and the lead roof.*

Buildings

The ubiquitous garden shed is seldom an attractive structure in its own right. As a result it tends to be tucked away in some dark corner of the garden. Should you be lucky enough to come across a structure which could fulfil the utilitarian role of a shed and yet be a decorative feature at the same time, it would be well worth the aggravation of transporting and resiting it.

It does not really matter if your new acquisition is not entirely in keeping with the architecture of your house. In the garden you can afford to have a bit of fun and enjoy a little fantasy. Siting the building amongst a grove of trees or behind some tall-growing shrubs will add a mysterious air, as well as helping to blend it into the framework of the garden.

You could utilize various salvaged elements and combine them to create a building. The small greenhouse pictured below falls into this category; I needed to give winter protection to my more tender plants but

did not like any of the conventional modern structures, nor was I prepared to incur the expense of building a traditional glazed-and-stone structure. I had some old window frames lying around so, with the help of a builder, I designed a structure around them.

The height of the garden wall against which it leans was a limiting factor, as it reduced the pitch of the roof to an unacceptable level. Instead of increasing the height in the centre of the greenhouse to create a long slope on one side and a shorter one near the wall, I put a wide, chunky shelf at each end to hide the roof line and the polycarbonate roof. It also created a useful space for storing pots (see photograph below).

WINDOWS

Good gardens are often made up of a series of successful spaces and the boundaries between them afford exciting design opportunities. I once saw a very good

RIGHT *My greenhouse was made by using reject window frames built on top of a stone wall. The roof is formed from polycarbonate insulated roofing sheets, which are only visible from inside the building. The slope of the roof is minimal as it is determined by the height of the adjacent wall. This looked unattractive so we made a chunky wooden shelf which disguises the mean pitch. The green opaque woodstain used was Jotun's 5816-G39Y.*

BELOW *This cupola with its bright gold finials at Elsing Hall makes an enchanting formal statement in the wilder part of the garden. The finials were salvaged from a building and used to great effect.*

Furniture

ABOVE *This old sink is in my kitchen garden, where it is used as a mini potting bench.*

RIGHT *Two good examples of ammonites salvaged by Bas Clarke and displayed in an unusual small stone trough which he keeps full of water to encourage birds to visit.*

BELOW *This raised trough made from a selection of salvaged stone and slate is at Plas Brondanw in North Wales, the gardens the late Sir Clough Williams-Ellis created around his own home. They are a fine example of his highly creative landscape design.*

FAR RIGHT *A stone mill wheel is raised on a base to come into service as a table.*

Stylish garden furniture can be very expensive, and salvage offers an attractive alternative that allows you to achieve individuality without breaking the bank.

PAINTED KITCHEN FURNITURE

Junk shops are excellent sources for old kitchen chairs and tables which only need to have a bit of paint or wood stain on them to have a new lease of life. Even if they are not made of hardwood, once they are coated they will last a good 10 years or so, especially if you bring them indoors in the winter.

In a smart London garden I once saw a simple wooden farmhouse table which had been painted a rich creamy yellow. Ranged around it were slatted wooden chairs which had been given a face-lift with a coat of bright green paint. The colour combination was unique and especially effective.

Old dressers, cupboards, chests of drawers, benches and settles can be treated in the same way and then put to good use, either outdoors or in a conservatory or potting shed. This is particularly useful in town gardens where space is at a premium.

CHURCH PEWS

Old church pews are very adaptable and are ideal additions to eating areas as well as being functional and

decorative on their own. Use a sander or a varnish remover to strip them of their old layers of varnish or polish and then prime and paint them or just seal the wood with a clear sealant.

OTHER SALVAGE MATERIAL

Tables and benches can be cobbled together from old stone. In the photograph below a stone mill wheel has been converted into a table. A huge reclaimed stone slab could be raised up on stone piers to form an unusual table, though you will not be able to move it very easily.

Large flag stones cut to size and propped up on two or three stone balls make excellent garden benches. A huge plank of wood, with narrow timber trunks screwed to the underside to form the legs, makes an ideal rustic table.

Old clinker boats have been revamped into arbours and seats, while salvaged animal troughs make excellent raised planters. Stone sinks can be converted into barbecues and potting benches or just resited to make useful outside sinks with taps for washing vegetables. Staddlestones, formerly used to raise agricultural buildings such as chicken sheds and granaries off the ground in order to prevent rats and mice from reaching the corn, are ideal decorative markers to define a grass edge along a driveway.

Sculptors

PETER GOUGH

Peter Gough salvages flint from the freshly ploughed fields of the South Downs. He sticks it together using an epoxy resin to create life-like figures in reclining, watching and leaning poses. He does not sketch his initial ideas but lets the shape of the flint guide him in forming the characteristics of his figures. Every piece is chosen with great care. If there is a missing part, it is left incomplete until the right shape comes to hand.

DAVID WILLIAMS

David Williams is a woodcarver and glass-engraver. He works predominantly with salvaged material, and as he is based in a studio on the banks of the River Wye, much of his raw material is washed up by the river. He carves pieces of driftwood into shapes inspired by Celtic legends, myths and biblical themes. A more recent inspirational source is the Adirondak style and he now produces furniture and buildings in this style.

IVAN HICKS

Ivan Hicks is a garden designer who strives to enhance the natural harmony and atmosphere he finds in a garden. Instead of drawing up formal plans, he gathers reclaimed objects, which vary from flints, pebbles and mirrors to old typewriters and parts of agricultural implements, and then arranges them to great effect, so that they become the structural framework of a garden.

RIGHT Peter Gough's sculpture, made of salvaged flints, has great energy and humanity.

BELOW RIGHT Old agricultural machinery can be a source of interesting salvaged finds. These discs from an old plough form a strong graphic statement in Ivan Hicks's garden.

BELOW LEFT David Williams created this building from pieces of timber which the river brought to his waterside studio.

His personal design motif is a spiral, representing eternity, evolution and immortality. He incorporates it in different ways: as mounds, in an arrangement of pebbles on the ground, or as a sculpture made from young coppiced material.

buildings
& accessories

 NO GARDEN IS EVER STATIC, BUT WHEN YOU REACH THE POINT WHERE AREAS ARE BEGINNING TO GEL – WHEN YOUR HEDGES ARE LIKE PROPER HEDGES AND THAT NEW, RAW LOOK HAS LEFT FOR GOOD – IT IS AN IDEAL TIME TO START THINKING ABOUT FURTHER EMBELLISHMENT. SOMETIMES WHEN YOU VISIT A HOUSE YOU CAN CHART THE OWNERS' TRAVELS AND ACQUIRE A GLIMPSE OF THEIR PAST LIVES THROUGH-OUT THE RANGE OF OBJECTS THAT ARE SCATTERED THROUGHOUT THEIR HOME. IT IS THE SAME WITH GARDENS WHICH VIVIDLY EXPRESS ELEMENTS OF THEIR CREATOR'S PERSONALITY. THE IMPACT ON A GARDEN OF BUILDINGS, FURNITURE, SCULPTURE AND EVEN CONTAINERS CAN BE GREAT, SO CARE NEEDS TO BE TAKEN IN THEIR SELECTION. WHEN SUCCESSFUL THEY ADD POLISH AND FOCUS.

Garden buildings

Most gardens need a building, even if it is just to store the lawn mower, pots and tools. However, over and above the purely functional, garden buildings also greatly enhance the look of a garden and the way that it is used. A conservatory can be used to grow more tender specimens, a gazebo provides a peaceful setting to admire a fine view and a simple summerhouse can be made into a quiet place in which to work undisturbed.

The eighteenth-century landscape gardens of England boast a range of buildings in their gardens: temples, follies, loggias, pavilions, orangeries, boat houses, hermitages and ruins. They are an integral part of the garden, defining the character of different areas and providing somewhere to 'walk to' or explore. Today, garden buildings are just as important. They tend to be relatively large compared to the size of the garden in which they stand and often fulfil many functions.

Whatever your use for the building, its other real function (and sometimes its sole function) is decorative. Make sure it has a definite style and choose the materials, site and size so that it really works.

SUITING THE BUILDING TO THE GARDEN

The most original and successful gardens are usually achieved by developing or emphasizing some unusual or positive attributes of the site. The same technique can be applied to designing a garden building and siting it appropriately. The ideal, of course, is a building that looks at one with the garden and not like a ready-made appendage that has been erected in the first available corner.

In one example that I designed recently the client had a small but well-proportioned walled kitchen garden. By tucking a stone building into the corner we maximized the area left as garden and made a feature of the curved stone walling, windows and doorways. The intrinsic charm of that garden lies in the strength of the walls surrounding it. By joining the building to the walls, it looks like an integral part of the garden and the strong, solid look is reinforced.

FINDING THE BEST FLOOR LEVEL

The level at which you site a garden building relative to the surrounding levels affects the way that it works in the context of the rest of the garden. For the small medieval-style building I made for the Chelsea Flower Show 1998, I sunk the building 18cm (7in) into the ground. This meant that you stepped down into it, which made it seem part of the double stairs, courtyard and rest of the garden.

The two-storey shed-cum-playhouse (see page 141 inset) was sunk 50cm (1ft 8in) to lessen its dominance in such a tiny space. However, if you wish to get an elevated feel and make the building seem more prominent and important you can raise it out of the ground and put steps up to it.

ABOVE *This charming tent adds an unusual focal point in the wild meadow area of the garden of landscape architect Tom Stuart-Smith. It is stoutly made from a timber roof which sits on a square framework of scaffold bars, which are in turn supported by four vertical scaffold bars. The fabric is held in place with velcro so it can easily be removed in winter.*

RIGHT *This simple timber building has been designed and sited with much care, forming a delightful punctuation mark in the middle of a long border. The all-important steep pitch of the roof is 51½ degrees, which sets it apart from the ordinary. The front of the building is clad with vertically hung cedar shingles. It is at The Old Vicarage, East Ruston.*

FAR RIGHT *The clear view through this magnificent building gives a translucent feel, anchoring it into the garden. It has high light levels inside with low window sills which allow the garden to spill into view. It was designed and made by Richard Foxcroft (see Suppliers' Guide).*

Style of building

Because of the smaller scale of many gardens today, the elaborate temples, columns, towers and grottoes that the eighteenth-century landscape designers so enjoyed would be far too grand for most situations. An informal, rustic approach is more easily accommodated in the more relaxed parts of contemporary gardens.

Grander and more formal garden buildings still have a place, particularly when adjacent to the house, formal swimming pool areas or paved terraces. However, quirky buildings or complete 'one-offs' that defy categorization, such as the gypsy caravan (see page 88) are increasing in popularity.

RUSTIC BUILDINGS

Rustic finishes blend happily into bosky, woodland settings. There are many different wall and roof finishes which fit into this category. Some, such as the interlocking jigsaw effect of peeled timber pieces which clads part of one of the two buildings at The Menagerie (see below) is a fascinating, decorative finish.

These two buildings are beautifully and meticulously detailed throughout and each one has three separate entrances, all totally different and leading from three totally different gardens. The Gothic arched doorway is clad with small-section wands of timber, as are the door and some of the furniture inside. These two buildings illustrate a few of the more unusual finishes achievable with wood.

An easier way to achieve a rustic effect is by cladding the walls (which could be marine ply) with round sections of timber fitted together in the same way as log round paving. Use different-sized rounds with many smaller ones so you can fit them together to cover as much of the material you are cladding as possible. Stain the finish to be clad with a dark organic colour using a translucent woodstain and either let the log rounds weather naturally, paint them with turpentine/linseed oil mix (see page 34), or stain them.

A more conventional finish is to use either horizontal or vertical timber boarding. Either of these could be mixed with one of the more decorative timber-finished panels, perhaps using the elaborate finishes around the doors and windows and the simpler finish on the corners. If you do work with the boarding, broad boards, about 30cm (1ft) wide, tend to look better than narrow ones.

ABOVE *At the Menagerie in Northamptonshire, two splendid garden buildings have been interestingly designed. A door has been clad with close-fitting, small-section birch branches, forming a warm-coloured and fascinating finish. The smoothness of the door contrasts strongly with the roughness of the bark-clad frame.*

RIGHT *On the exterior of the building rough finish made from bark cladding is fitted together rather like a mosaic. In another section, the bark cladding conceals a secret door which is indistinguishable from the surrounding frame, the handle too being clad with bark.*

FAR RIGHT *A different view of the building at The Menagerie pictured right. The uprights formed from medium-sized timbers support a heavy thatch overhang which covers a small sun-drenched sitting area overlooking a huge pool. The small seat has been designed to incorporate the same birch detailing that is on the door.*

Ben Wilson's Rustic Buildings

Ben Wilson is a sculptor who creates a wide range of timber pieces that include intriguing buildings and sculptures which respond to, and seem almost to grow out of, their environment. The building shown on this page is formed predominantly from reclaimed wood — discarded scaffold planks, beach driftwood, brushwood, a tree that has been blown down in a storm and would otherwise be burnt, timber from skips, rubbish dumps and graveyards.

To maximize the life of the wood and to obtain the soft shapes, unless the timber is of a very small, twiggy size Ben removes the bark from the tree with a draw knife which helps to reduce the rate at which the timber disintegrates. For most types of wood this is easier to do when the bark is still wet with sap. Some timbers are much more difficult to peel the bark off than others: beech, for example, is particularly awkward but ash is much easier.

Ben lets his work evolve spontaneously from the timber he happens to come across and from his reactions to the site where they are going to stand. The natural imperfections in the timbers — the knots, hollows and curves — are the variations he exploits to make the structures come alive. Mosses, fungi, birds' nests and beetles all add to the richness of the art and ensure that each piece is highly individual.

Ben uses basic tools such as an adze, which is similar to an axe but has an arched blade at the top at right angles to the handle. He uses it to pull the wood on the line of the grain, to form the shapes he wants. Other simple tools he uses are axes, saws, hammers and sometimes nails, though he tries to avoid the latter; knowing that his work will slowly break down over the years, he prefers to introduce as few alien items as possible.

His work is distinctive and firmly rooted in the natural world, with images of trees, plants, animals and the landscape coming through strongly.

RIGHT *This arbour has been made from salvaged timber by Ben Wilson (see Suppliers' Guide). The curving patterns cut out of the timber are a feature of Ben's work, giving it a very organic feel.*

MUD, STRAW AND OTHER RUSTIC FINISHES

Cob buildings used to be made from mud and straw, and the technique is still occasionally used today by specialists. Keen amateurs can experiment with these materials to create very rustic buildings.

To start the construction you need a low plinth for the walls to sit on to raise them out of the damp. This can be formed from brick, stone or concrete and should be about 15cm (6in) above ground level. The usual method of building is to make a timber frame for the walls, and then weave willow or hazel branches through the frame to provide a base for the mud mix to cling to.

The main stage of work – the packing with mud – must be done during a warm, preferably dry, period so the walls can dry out before being subjected to long periods of heavy rain. To make the mix you need a soil with about 25 per cent clay and a high content of coarse sand, gravel or stone. The subsoil is mixed with straw and water and packed onto the timberwork.

The finished walls can be either fairly smooth or very uneven, creating a homespun look. The roof should overhang the walls by a good depth, at least 30cm (1ft), to keep them as dry as possible. Thatch, reed, straw and sedge look well with the organic colour of the dry mud (which will vary from area to area), as do timber shingles and clay or stone tiles. Cob walls are ideal for forming into curves, either for archways over doors and windows or for the layout of the walls.

WILLOW HOUSES

Willow can be woven into wonderfully sculptural shapes to form small garden buildings which, because of their highly organic nature, instantly fit in and become part of the landscape. Simple versions of these are fairly easy to make yourself (see page 115). Otherwise, if you want a work of art, call in one of the few specialist willow sculptors such as Clare Wilks (see Suppliers' Guide).

FORMAL GARDEN BUILDINGS

Formal buildings may be any style, perhaps designed to go with the house, or they may be a separate entity elsewhere in the garden and not intended to relate to anything. If you are considering a structure such as those illustrated here, it is worth bringing in the experts and choosing an architect whose work you admire to

ABOVE *I designed this building to sit on stilts in the water, surrounded by lavish water plants, for the Chelsea Flower Show 1996. The roof is made from sedge thatch, which is far easier and cheaper to use than straw or reed thatch, as can be seen from the step-by-step tree house on page 97. The whitewash covered timber combined with distressed blue louvred doors gives the building a tropical feel.*

RIGHT *This recently built formal garden building has two open sides to make the most of the dramatic views over the valley. The intricate stone opening allows glimpses of the borders behind. Note the relatively steep pitch of the Collyweston stone roof.*

design it for you. This way you will be sure to get the right effect and the necessary consistency of detailing on aspects such as materials, windows, roof pitches and entrances, as well as overall size and proportion. Most of the examples here were designed either by architects or landscape architects.

QUIRKY BUILDINGS

If you want to have a really unusual hideaway the garden is one place where you can often accommodate more outlandish types of buildings – and you have the opportunity to re-create, if necessary, surroundings that can show them off to their best advantage.

Aviaries are fascinating buildings for a garden and they are fairly easy to site as they are visually very light. Their unique function also adds to their appeal. For less mobile people, an aviary can be a constant source of interest if it is sited so that it can be viewed from a window of the house.

Aviaries are not just sophisticated cages for birds – they can also be designed for free-flying flocks, for example, certain types of budgerigars can be managed so that they will fly in and out of their aviaries at will, generally spending the day loose in the garden and returning to the aviary at night. Budgerigars can live outside in an aviary in England provided they have a covered space which is dark and sheltered.

The door of an aviary should be designed to stop the birds flying out when you go in. This can be done by splitting the door in half, making in effect two half doors, so that you only open the bottom half to go in and out, and duck under the top half. Birds do not swoop down to fly out.

A more complicated way to keep the birds in when you enter or leave is to have two doors with a gap between, enabling you to open just one at a time. This is a lot more cumbersome to design, as the doors need bigger timber or metal supports.

BELOW LEFT *This dramatic building was designed and bult by Richard Foxcroft. It is a conservatory which uses rustic shaped timbers and small areas of coloured glass. The wall at the base, with its naturally curved oak coping, combines well with the overall curved shape of the structure.*

BELOW RIGHT *I designed this small aviary with its runs leading off the back specially for free-flying budgerigars. These lucky birds are allowed out to fly around during the day and return to the aviary at night.*

Sculpture

Garden design is extending its horizons, and many craftspeople, artists, photographers, painters, architects and sculptors are becoming increasingly involved in working in the garden environment, adding new and exciting influences to it.

Sculpture is making a strong contribution to garden design and draws upon a wide range of media, including wood, ceramics, bronze, glass, stainless steel, stone, GRP and wrought iron. If you want to start adding this dimension to your garden but are not familiar with the many different media and forms, visit some sculpture gardens and parks (see Suppliers' Guide) where you will see the work of a wide range of artists and, just as important, the different styles, materials and ways the sculptures are sited in garden situations.

At Hannah Peschar's sculpture garden near Ockley in Surrey, you can see 40 to 50 different artists' work in a superb garden setting. The garden has been redesigned by the garden designer Anthony Paul, who has replanted it over the past 20 years, creating a superb setting for a wide range of sculpture. Hannah Peschar is keen to make sculpture more accessible to everyone and will offer advice on how to site sculpture and make it work in the garden context.

Art is often classified as abstract and figurative but these definitions are not helpful when applied to work which falls into both categories. For this reason I have used the terms referential, abstracted and abstract.

REFERENTIAL SCULPTURE

Referential sculpture is usually the first type of sculpture we appreciate early on in life. There are many pieces of this type, such as the fantastic bird pictured below which is so arresting that I would never tire of looking at it.

ABSTRACTED SCULPTURE

Abstracted sculpture has a referential element to some degree but this may scarcely be apparent, depending on the individual style of the sculptor. Henry Moore is probably the best-known sculptor whose work falls into this category. It presents perhaps more of a challenge to the viewer than referential art and can be appreciated at different levels. The shapes and forms can be valued as they stand, with no further speculation about what they are meant to be, or you can ponder them further and start to understand and enjoy them at a deeper level.

ABSTRACT SCULPTURE

Differing from abstracted work in the fact that it does not emerge from a figurative base, abstract sculpture, with its emphasis on the qualities of colour, form, line and surface, can be used in garden settings to form a bold and exciting blend of art and nature. An exhilarating quality can be achieved by the introduction of an eye-catching work of art, especially when it is in a well-established framework of a garden, contrasting with buildings and plants that have been there for hundreds of years.

BRONZE

Bronze will last not just for a lifetime but for thousands of years and its very permanence is an integral part of its charm. It is a versatile metal which can take on different patinas and colours, according to its age and how the material is manipulated. The blue-grey colour of many bronzes is formed by brushing them with acid and then using a blow torch to oxidize the metal, pulling the copper tones out of it. Other colours, including greens, reds, whites, blues, browns and whites, can also be encouraged to take hold, although

they are not totally static and will slowly change over the years as oxidization continues.

Different casting techniques will also affect the final look of the bronze. Casting in sand does not produce deep relief and gives quite crude forms, whereas casting using the lost wax method can form sculpture with a detailed surface. Bronze is an expensive metal to work with and so, inevitably, this is reflected in the price of sculpture for sale.

STONE

Stone has been used in many different ways to adorn grand gardens for hundreds of years. It lends itself to all forms of sculpture and all varieties of buildings. There are many types of stone, each with their own character, that are suitable for the cool European climate, including granites, some marbles, slate, Portland stone and sandstones. The softer stones are easier to carve but do not have the same weather resistance as the harder ones.

WOOD

Many sculptors prefer to work with old salvaged timber, which has already done most of the twisting and moving it is going to. Often it will have blemishes from its past use which add to its charm. When huge blocks of wood are needed for the raw material it is often impractical to use anything other than green wood, as the process of drying out is so difficult. Sometimes green oak or elm are used, both of which can move and split, although this too can add extra character to the finished sculpture.

Timber is more commonly used by sculptors than bronze or stone because of its lower cost and easy availability. However, some woods, particularly softwoods, are fairly short-lived, although there are a few exceptionally durable timbers such as bog oak.

CERAMICS

Ceramic sculptures which will be subjected to frost need to be fired at high temperatures (about 1260°C, at which temperature the clay vitrifies). If they are then glazed and fired again they become particularly tough and are even suitable for use in water features.

BELOW LEFT *This dramatic sculpture is sited on the edge of Ian Hamilton-Finlay's garden, Little Sparta, near Edinburgh. It is called 'The Present Order' and consists of 11 stones on which are carved a quotation from Saint Just. It was designed by Ian Hamilton-Finlay in collaboration with the sculptor, Nicholas Sloan.*

BELOW RIGHT *This oak abstracted sculpture is one of many exciting pieces at the Hannah Peschar Sculpture Garden (see Suppliers' Guide). It is by Walter Bailey and is entitled 'Skeletal Egg'.*

Plant containers

BELOW LEFT *These delicate wire plant stands are more commonly used to display plants indoors, but they are ideally suited for displaying interesting collections outside too. Here sedums and other drought-tolerant plants are shown to good advantage.*

BELOW CENTRE *In my own garden I tend to use pots in bold groups with simple, repeated planting in them. Here eight large Greek terracotta pots are filled with Prunus lusitanica (standard bay laurels) which, together with eight box balls planted directly in gravel, frame a walkway along the north side of our house.*

BELOW RIGHT *At Elton Hall these pots have been painted the same colour as the doors of the orangery — Farrow & Ball's Stone Blue No. 86. The quatrefoil on the containers has also been picked up from the orangery.*

Many gardeners love using pots and containers in their gardens because they are so versatile. Their position and contents can be altered from one season to the next to give a fresh look to a familiar space. They can indeed provide spectacular effects, particularly when they are integrated into the structure of the garden and not added in piecemeal fashion.

I like to use pots structurally, making them part of the framework of the garden by grouping them in lines, squares or patterns to strengthen a particular layout.

André Le Nôtre, the designer who laid out Versailles for Louis XIV, used pots in a structural way in many of the gardens he created. He would lead the eye down vistas and avenues by using large fruit trees in huge tubs. They introduced instant height at eye level as well as lots of initial impact to bring definition to the spectacular spaces he was generating. He tended to use the same style of pot and type of plant in one space to give a strong, cohesive feel.

This technique is equally valid today and is ideal for both geometric or informal designs. For it to be effective, use a single style of pot and planting and make the pots as large as your garden will take.

TYPES OF CONTAINER

Large pots need to look good and can be quite expensive. Instead of lavishing money on beautiful pale pinkish Italian terracotta or the etched pots from Greece, it is possible to improve the cheaper mass-produced terracotta

pots. One option is to weather them with limewash or alternatively paint them with a masonry paint such as Ointment Pink from Farrow & Ball and follow this with a weathered finish.

Timber Planters

Simple large timber planters could be made from marine ply, which could be transformed if required with a simple moulded frame fixed around the sides. The timber could be painted with an opaque woodstain. As the plant containers need to be structurally strong to take that much weight, it is worth taking a leaf out of the late David Hicks's book and using the timber container as an outer cladding with a less decorative plastic pot inside. This system also allows you to change the plants over with less effort, as plastic pots are lighter and therefore easier to move around.

Painted Plastic Pots

Plastic pots can be transformed by imaginative colours (see below right) or paint effects.

Galvanized Metal

Large galvanized metal containers can be formed from metal ducting or vent pipes, obtainable from steel pipe manufacturers. If you have a problem sourcing these you could get sheets of galvanized steel and get them rolled up into cylinders. With both these systems you would need to line them with a black polythene liner which has

drainage holes at the base. Or you can purchase ready-made large galvanized pots (see Suppliers' Guide).

Decorative Pots

Decorative pots are one of the most commonly used garden ornaments. They are effective either in collections of various shapes and sizes or used singly to form a focal point – for the latter you need an impressive large pot, for example an urn, works well. Study your garden to see where you can site the pots so that they will have the most impact. This may not necessarily be at the end of a vista or by doorways. They may look most effective within a plant border providing contrast against a clump of grasses or shrubs, for example.

Sometimes the container is meant to be unseen, leaving the planting to provide the stunning aspect. Alternatively, the pots themselves can provide the eye-catching element. Keep an eye out for the unusual and breathtaking, and start collecting them. To make more of a pot or trough, raise it up on a piece of stone or some tiles as everything is more noticeable when it is nearer eye level.

RIGHT *Contrasting modern galvanized plant containers give a bold new look to this traditional London terraced house. These containers are available from Stephen Woodhams (see Suppliers' Guide).*

Furniture

I like to have several 'furnished spaces' in a garden to entice people to stop and enjoy a particular area. The space may be tiny, with just one or two seats, or bigger, with expansive benches and tables. It is the furniture in a garden, as in a room, that really seems to emphasize the function of the space. It also brings out the personality of the garden. A group of very modern, beautifully designed furniture can contrast well against a traditional house and garden, in the same way as modern paintings can look stunning in a period setting inside the house. This is one area where a contrast of styles can give a fresh feel to a garden.

The problem with much of the garden furniture available is that you see it over and over again. Your garden will benefit greatly if you aim to find some furniture that is different and unusual. One way, if you have the budget, is to purchase limited-supply, upmarket, high-quality designs. Another is to find a craftsman whose style you appreciate. Alternatively, you can hunt around at house sales or even make your own which, provided you work out a simple design, should not be too difficult. As an intermediate step before taking on the full do-it-yourself option you could buy inexpensive mass-produced furniture and personalize it, perhaps by painting it or using attractive cushions.

There are many craftsmen who make rustic furniture from coppiced hazel, willow, sweet chestnut and other timbers. Many different styles can be formed and result in simple and interesting furniture that is reasonably priced because of the low cost of the material.

transforming
problem sites

IN MOST PROPERTIES THE HOUSE EXERTS CONSIDERABLE INFLUENCE ON THE GARDEN FROM AT LEAST ONE PERSPECTIVE. AS WELL AS FORMING THE BACKDROP AGAINST WHICH THE GARDEN IS VIEWED, IT ALSO PROVIDES SHELTERED AREAS AND TERRACED SPACES WHERE WE SPEND TIME RELAXING. FEW HOUSES, HOWEVER, ARE ARCHITECTURALLY PERFECT AND MOST ARE AFFLICTED BY VARIOUS EYESORES: VENT PIPES, CABLING, A FLAT ROOF, UNSYMPATHETIC ADDITIONS AND UGLY WINDOWS. TO MAKE THE MOST OF A GARDEN, AN EXCELLENT STARTING POINT IS TO TAKE A LONG HARD LOOK AT YOUR HOUSE AND BECOME FULLY ACQUAINTED WITH ALL ITS IMPERFECTIONS. THE SECOND STEP IS TO FIND REMEDIES WITHOUT INVOLVING MAJOR BUILDING WORKS, AND THAT IS WHERE THIS CHAPTER COMES IN.

Improving entrances & forecourts

The entrance to your house and the immediate garden surrounding it are the most often seen parts of a property. They determine the visitors' all-important first impressions as they arrive, and have a second impact as the last thing they see when they leave. The front door is usually the focal point of the entrance. Highlighting it further by putting a porch over it, adding collections of pots around it, or arranging well-detailed trellis either side of it, creates a welcoming focal point. If required, it can also distract the eye from less attractive features at the front of the house.

THE CEREMONY OF ARRIVAL

Some houses have striking entrances which make such a strong impact that they define henceforth the way that we think about the house and garden. Ignoring those that are impressive purely because they belong to buildings of great architectural importance, there are many more that are striking simply because of the individuality of their entrances and the way in which they create a 'sense of arrival'.

ABOVE *One of my favourite gardens, Plas Brondawnw, was the home of the late Sir Clough Williams-Ellis. This charming but unfussy courtyard is brightened up with splashes of his 'Portmeirion Green'. The huge standard bay trees define the entrance way and the old bell makes it clear to which door the visitor should go.*

RIGHT *At the Old Vicarage, East Ruston, the planting transforms this entrance to the property. The fastigiate conifers, the clipped holly hedge — complete with piers and balls — add grand 'green architectural features' to the house which create a real sense of arrival. The area in front of these formal elements, which is mostly out of shot, is a large expanse of gravel informally but densely planted with a range of low-level drought-resistant plants which contrast superbly with the more severe planting behind.*

A COTTAGE IN BUCKINGHAMSHIRE

This brick-built cottage is very long and thin. The garage, set back and at right angles to the house, was the first thing you used to see as you approached the property. The owner, landscape architect, Honor Gibbs, designed a porch/canopy to extend over the drive, with a small screened eating area tucked into the far end of it. This cleverly conceals part of the garage, and makes the drive very much part of the garden, by incorporating the eating area into the canopy. It breaks up the long thin elevation of the cottage, and makes a welcoming feature for both house and garden.

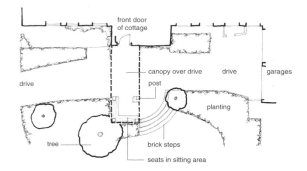

FIG. 26 *Honor Gibbs' driveway with canopies*

RIGHT *The plan above illustrates how Honor Gibbs has visually broken up the long elevation of her cottage by putting a canopy (right) across her drive and at right angles to the building. The canopy provides a sheltered eating area at one end and is an ingenious way to pull the drive into the garden while at the same time partially screening the view of the garage as you enter the property.*

ENTRANCES

Another striking entrance which has stuck in my mind is that of a town house in Marrakesh. All that can be seen from the street are the impenetrable walls with solid, wooden doors kept tightly shut. As you go through them, the entrance courtyard is full of bright colours — bold blue paintwork on the house, and an exuberance of luxuriant foliage clothing the perimeter walls. The design of the space is simple and bold, a well-proportioned rectangle with great planting. The impact lies in the contrast between the hot, brown, dusty, busy street and the lush green private tranquillity of the courtyard — the senses are totally shocked, in the nicest possible way.

It is not always possible to create such a vivid contrast between the outside world and your inner sanctuary, but each property will have some sort of quality that can be developed to provide both a distinctive and a welcoming entrance area to your home. For example,

RIGHT *At Anna Simond's house in France, strategically placed pots and swags of vine create a welcoming entrance to this cottage.*

BELOW LEFT *The cloistered calm of the courtyard at Tamy Tasi, Marrakesh.*

BELOW CENTRE *This bell looks most attractive surrounded by the neat box hedge. It was designed by Michael Balston.*

BELOW RIGHT *This charming entrance which is heavily adorned with rampant climbers and well-cherished plants in pots, immediately imparts a welcoming feeling to the visitor. It also functions well, forming a relaxed and sheltered space in which to greet your guests.*

a formal symmetrical avenue can form a superbly elegant approach but the building at the end must match in terms of elegance and symmetry. If your property is a cosy-looking cottage, a gently curving approach with perhaps a few native trees planted in grassy verges would be far more appropriate.

The siting of a huge bell in an entrance area (see page 156) provides an excellent focal point which also serves a useful function. The positioning of the bell forces you to slow down and go through the ritual of ringing it, which then becomes a unique part of the arrival process at this particular house.

DISGUISING DRIVEWAYS

The size of an entrance area must be in proportion to the size of the house. A large tall house should ideally have a sizeable space or the entrance will look out of balance. Parked cars often dominate the front of a house. Ideally they should be discreetly tucked to one side, so they are out of sight of the main entrance, and don't detract from its appearance. If you do not have garaging, try to screen the main parking area with planting or walling. Sometimes a heavily planted pergola works well, and in hot summers it also provides useful shade.

The surfacing provides further opportunities for enhancing an entrance area. First consider the shape: the space you need for easy vehicular access need not be conventional hammerhead shape. Geometrical designs such as rectangles, circles, squares and ovals can successfully disguise the area's primary function. Emphasize the pleasing

outline with bands of a paving material such as flags or granite setts and plant trees, topiary or decorative hedging to further reinforce their shape. If you are worried about plants being a hazard, use cones to mark their intended position and see how that works for a few weeks.

ABOVE RIGHT Here at Stapleford Park, my client wanted to discourage people from parking their cars right up against the building, which ruined the views to and from it. So I designed two parterres either side of the front door, these depict the points of the compass in one and the symbols of the four local hunts in the other. The gravel is used as a mulch for the hedging and hides a polythene weed barrier, but it also pulls together the hedging and the driveway. The stone balls physically prevent cars from damaging the hedging. The photograph was taken twelve months after planting. Buxus sempervirens (common box) was chosen rather than Buxus suffructicosa (edging box) to give a more instant and robust effect.

BELOW RIGHT (FIGS 27 & 28) A driveway is normally treated as a functional area for parking and turning a car round in. It also usually forms the foreground to your property and so often is a key item which determines the overall impression of the house and garden. It creates a more restful appearance if it is a static space, not long and narrow in shape, as that would have the undesired effect of drawing you on through the area. To this end it often works better if the drive in front of the house is of generous proportions. Fig 28 is a plan of a driveway which provides a very basic but functional space. Fig 27 shows an extended drive which is more restful, like a courtyard. I have included some paving in the centre and around the edge to break up the gravel and reinforce the shape. Trees and box balls are planted in the hard area in a formal fashion, and other more informal plants can be placed in the gravel around the edges.

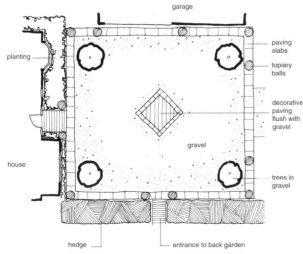

FIG. 27 *Drive design providing attractive courtyard entrance*

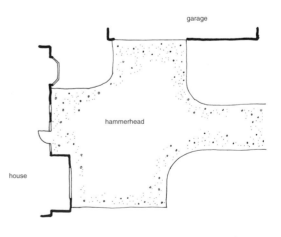

FIG. 28 *Utilitarian drive with turning hammerhead*

Disguising a flat roof

Flat roofs are one of the most commonly found eye-sores: they are often tacked on as late additions to a property with insufficient attention paid to the blending of architectural styles. A traditional way to hide one is to put a parapet or low wall above the gutter line all around the edge. Depending on the sightlines, it may not be necessary to take the wall around all four sides. Parapet walls can be finished with coping or perhaps embellished with crenellations or finials (these will not suit every style of building). A stone balustrade topped with a coping is also successful in some situations. Balustrading comes in many different styles, and the simpler ones such as stone latticing are more compatible than the elaborate ones. Orangeries – the elegant 'gar-den rooms' that are a feature of grand stately homes – often have elegant urns in a line on top of their walls. Re-creating this style on a more down-to-earth scale can be achieved with a decorative line of simple large pots or stone balls.

Screening with planting is often the most economical way of concealing a flat roof. It is usually the continu-ous straight line just above eye level that needs hiding,

so small trees which reach high enough to break it up are ideal. The trees should be planted fairly close to the edge of the building in strong geometric groups at close centres. Ideally, repeat this grouping somewhere else close by so that a pattern develops within the garden and it is less obvious that the trees are there purely to hide something ugly.

USING PERGOLAS OR COLONNADES

Pergolas are another useful means of deflecting the eye from a flat roof and ugly fascia boards – and indeed many other eyesores. They need to be at the same height as the roof, so a relatively low building such as a garage would be a suitable candidate for the treatment. Build the per-gola with broad horizontal beams so that the roof line is hidden and ideally try to integrate some sort of link with the house, making it modern or traditional, plain or ornate as appropriate. Climbing plants will also, of course, help the pergola to fit into its environment. Alternatively, colonnades formed from plants have a soft-er look than pergolas, and will combine well with any type of architecture (see page 112).

RIGHT *My tiny walled garden was dominated by a neigh-bour's flat-roofed extension built in the 1960s. I decided to remove it visually with these pleached hornbeams. They were planted as transplants, a maxi-mum of 600mm (2ft) high, about six years ago and now they frame the two long sides, almost obscuring the eyesore.*

Disguising garden essentials

Most properties have unattractive but essential fixtures such as oil and gas tanks, large vent pipes, hose reels, ugly windows or lengths of unattractive walling, to name but a few. Plant-clad trellises and timber batten screens are good solutions for hiding all sorts of unattractive garden essentials.

COLOUR DISGUISES

Before thinking about screening, make sure you have tried camouflaging with colour first – or perhaps you may need to use both. Colour can be a great help in making offending items such as large oil tanks merge into the background (see page 16).

ABOVE *Instead of using the standard metal posts to fence his tennis court, Michael Balston has employed hefty timber verticals and horizontals to which he has fixed almost invisible netting to catch the balls. The picture shows the recently completed work. Imagine it a few months down the line when the climbers have established over the pergola.*

RIGHT TOP *This small coke bunker has been camouflaged by cleverly detailed trellis designed by the Keyes brothers.*

FAR RIGHT TOP *Shelves and beautifully arranged pots and plants transform this simple potting shed.*

RIGHT BELOW *A bold white modern bin store, photographed with the gate open in order to prove the point!*

FAR RIGHT BELOW *Another camouflaged compost bin, this time using more traditional hazel hurdles and a planted wigwam.*

Softening walls

PLANTS

Plants are regularly used to adorn walls, and they not only help pull together the building and garden but also make disparate elements of a garden more cohesive. Think carefully about the style of the property and choose appropriate plants. For example, barn conversions can look fussy covered with lots of flowering climbers but trained fruit trees look particularly good against the dark timber weatherboarding and suit the rural context.

To make an even stronger impact, climbers, shrubs and trees can be trained into unusual forms. Fruit trees, such as apples, peaches, apricots and cherries, can form espaliers, fans or palmettes.

Climbers can be trained to form virtually any shape: they can arch over ground-floor and first-floor windows in a figure-of-eight shape, fill a section of wall with diagonal crossing lattice, form links of a chain running along a wall, or create repetitive rectangular panels. Making patterns obviously takes time, but initially a specially designed trellis of bold proportions can provide the framework and expectation of glories to come. To minimize the time you have to spend on clipping your elaborate shapes, choose slow-growing evergreens such as *Pyracantha* species, *Trachelospermum jasminoides* and certain types of ivies, such as *Hedera helix* 'Cristata' and *H. h.* 'Atropurpurea'.

GREEN BUTTRESSES

Plants that respond well to trimming can be planted right up against a wall and trained on it so that they make living green buttresses. These are a stylish but simple method to break up a monotonous stretch of walling. Plants that can be used in this way include *Taxus baccata* (common yew), *T. b.* 'Fastigiata' (Irish yew), *Laurus nobilis* (sweet bay), *Buxus sempervirens* (box) and *Pittosporum tenuifolium*.

SHROUDS

If the building is generally not to your liking, the best thing to do is to almost totally shroud it in foliage. It is a bold approach which, on the occasions that I have seen it done, works very successfully. Only allow glimpses of the parts of the house which you are happy to show, and ensure the rest is covered. In this way all the emphasis will shift from the architecture to the planting.

RIGHT *An impenetrable high wall that could look oppressive has been softened by the planting.*

FAR RIGHT *At Deene Park in Northamptonshire, these cleanly shaped green buttresses made from box are another excellent example of green architecture. Here their function is to visually divide the long length of house and break up the plant bed into smaller chunks. To do this they are used at equal-spaced intervals.*

RIGHT *No prizes for guessing where this is – the Portmeirion Green gives the game away. Here the late Sir Clough Williams-Ellis has introduced this bright and ornate barge board to decorate an otherwise bland end elevation.*

PAINT EFFECTS

Paint finishes provide a fast and relatively cheap means of livening up a dull façade. Stone-blocking a nondescript rendered wall or finishing it with a tinted limewash will start to bring the surface alive, for example. For the more committed, a small trompe l'oeil, such as a sundial, can add further interest. (See pages 26–45 for further information.)

ENHANCING GOOD FEATURES

Once you have made the most of the good features of your house, and disguised the bad ones as much as possible, you can work on further embellishments that might serve a particular purpose, define a space more effectively, or simply add an element of fun. Timber or metal structures have great potential: they might be designed to form a covered area, raised platform, veranda, gallery or pergola.

ABOVE *This basement entrance was not prominent enough and so was given a canopy over the door complete with bold finial to draw attention to it. Designed by Michael Balston.*

ABOVE RIGHT *These columns in Ian Hamilton-Finlay's garden have been formed by painted stucco and totally transform this previously simple building and the entire space around it. The lettering adds further interest.*

RIGHT *A raised decking area adjacent to an old Cotswold Mill gives wonderful views over a small walled space. The structure, together with the surrounding dense planting, lifts the house, creating an unusual but highly usable space. It was designed and built by Mike Harvey (see Suppliers' Guide).*

Awnings

Awnings and canopies are currently enjoying a revival, partly perhaps because of increased concern about the harmful effects of over-exposure to the sun, but also because people enjoy the way their instant injection of colour livens up a terrace, entrance or sitting area. Awnings project much further out than canopies, and form an area of shade under which one can sit. Canopies usually measure only about 60cm–1.2m (2–4ft) wide and are designed primarily to prevent the sun from invading a room.

MATERIALS

Awnings are usually made from an acrylic version of canvas which has been treated to be showerproof. Ordinary canvas can be used, but it will rot more quickly and you need to take it down when it rains. Other fabrics are available, such as shiny 'wet-look' ones. Fabric awnings are available in a vast range of patterns: bold stripes or single colours are usually better than ornate ones, which tend to look too fussy. Bright primary colours give a sophisticated, urban and modern look. Greens, browns, soft yellows and muted blues give a calm, subtle feel. Plain white goes with everything and doesn't fade.

Moving away from fabric entirely, bamboo awnings look wonderful with modern buildings. Coppiced hazel and other woods are ideal where a rustic effect is required but even then are best kept for small areas.

Awning manufacturers now make automatic models that zoom in and out at the touch of a button. The traditional ones are wound by hand into a cassette. If you are making your own awning supports, make sure they look good without the fabric cover as you will see a lot of them in winter. Hazel, reed and bamboo supports can be left out all year round.

Linking disparate elevations

Many houses have been added to over a period of time, often in a variety of different styles and materials, which leaves them looking fragmented. Quite often, minor alterations to windows, doors and wall finishes, together with prominent and repetitive use of bold planting, can have a dramatically unifying effect.

The example shown on this page is a small cottage, which was probably originally a dovecote, built in the eighteenth century. Its original features are quite charming: a pyramid roof, pleasing square proportions and well-detailed stonework. Unfortunately in the early 1960s a large flat-roofed extension was added at the back, with a huge obtrusive chimney and aerial looming above it. Inappropriate windows, out of keeping with the old part of the house, were fitted throughout the building. Red gas bottles were fixed to the front elevation, though fortunately they were partly obscured by laurel bushes, and glazed lights were set into the main front door.

When you arrived at the house, all these ugly features greeted you. Restoring the composition to near what it once was involved making all the 1960s alterations recede and the old, attractive features stand out.

To this end the windows and doors on the old part of the house were painted to match the other domestic dwellings in the farmyard. The lower windows also had thin beading added onto the glass.

On the extension, the windows, doors and fascia board were painted the same colour as the stone of the old part, and so receded into the background. A timber screen, complete with bun-turned posts with stop chamfers, and heavy trelliswork were used to mask the extensive roof. The timber had to be chunky to remain in keeping with the solid architecture of the cottage; the bun twists give a Jacobean look, while the vertical bars at the top of the trellis were reminiscent of a stable partition – appropriate to the converted farmyard setting. The trellis screen had the added bonus of forming a west-facing sitting area behind it, which has become a small semi-private courtyard that gets the dappled evening sun. The red gas bottles were tucked in behind the new screen and the walls of the extension were covered by extensive planting to provide a pleasant backdrop to the newly enclosed area. Sturdy but decorative planting highlights the front door, allowing the old front elevation of the dovecot to assume greater prominence.

BELOW *This cottage was originally a building of quality, but the flat-roofed extension together with the alterations which introduced these enlarged and discordant windows turned it into an eyesore.*

RIGHT *To try to improve its appearance without resorting to a wrecking ball, I painted all the ugly timber features on the recessed elevation (windows, lintels, doors and fascia board) a dark stone colour to make them less prominent. I then screened this part by putting in the heavy trellis structure. I have added false beading to some windows to break up the large panes and some windows have been changed. The trellis was painted with Sadolin's Superdec Jungle Green, the finials picked out in Fali Straw. Planting will be used to soften the whole effect.*

List of suppliers

LANDSCAPE ARTISTS & GARDEN DESIGNERS
Bonita Bulaitis, 6 Watton Road, Ware, Hertfordshire SG12 OAA
Tel 01920 466466

Bunny Guinness, Landscape Architect, Sibberton Lodge, Thornhaugh, Peterborough PE8 6NH
Tel & fax 01780 782518

Christopher Bradley-Hole Ltd, Studio 10, Sutton Lane North, London W4 4LD
Tel 0181 742 1867

Fiona Lawrenson, Floribunda, Thursley Lodge, Farnham Lane, Haslemere, Surrey GU27 1HA
Tel 01428 651776

Honor Gibbs, Landscape Architect, Environmental Design Associates, 89 Bicester Road, Long Crendon, Aylesbury, Buckinghamshire HP18 9EF
Tel 01844 208418

Ivan Hicks, Landscape Architect, Garden in Mind, Stanstead Park, Hampshire
Tel 01705 413149

Michael Balston, Landscape Architect, Balston & Company, Long Barn, Patney, Devizes, Wiltshire SN10 3RB
Tel 01380 848 181 Fax 01380 848189

Peter Styles, Landscape Architect, Lingard & Styles Landscape, Walpole House, 35 Walpole Street, London SW3 4QS
Tel 0171 730 9233 Fax 0171 730 9152

Siddeley Landscapes Ltd, 2 Palmerston Court, Palmerston Way, London SW8 4AJ
Tel 0171 6277200 Fax 0171 6277201

LANDSCAPE CONTRACTORS
Steve Hooper Landscapes, 6 Barrington Court, Crouch End, London N8 8QS
Tel 0181 340 6041

PAINTS AND WOODSTAINS
Farrow & Ball, Uddens Estate, Wimborne, Dorset BH21 7NL
Tel 01202 876141 Fax 01202 873793

Fired Earth plc, Twyford Mill, Oxford Road, Adderbury, Oxfordshire OX17 3HP
Tel 01295 812088 Fax 01295 810832

Jane Churchill range from Farrow & Ball.

Jotun-Henry Clark Decorative Paints, Alston Drive, Bradwell Abbey, Milton Keynes MK13 9HA
Tel 01908 321818 Fax 01908 315073

Johnstone's Paints, Huddersfield Road, Birstall, Batley, West Yorkshire WF17 9XA
Tel 01924 354000

Limewash and traditional building limes: Hirst Conservation Materials, Laughton, Sleaford, Lincs NG34 0HE
Tel 01529 497517 Fax 01529 497518

Papers and Paints Ltd, 4 Park Walk, London SW10
Tel 0171 352 8626 Fax 0171 352 1017

Sadolin UK Ltd, Sadolin House, Meadow Lane, St Ives, Cambridgeshire PE17 4UY
Tel 01480 496868 Fax 01480 496801

ARTISTS FOR PAINT EFFECTS
Martin T. Rodgers, 6 Old North Road, Wansford, Peterborough PE8 6LB
Tel 01780 751544/01780 782007

WROUGHT IRON WORK
Fotheringhay Forge, The Forge, Fotheringhay, Oundle, Peterborough
Tel 01832 226323

GOLD LEAF SUPPLIERS
L. Cornelissen and Sons Ltd, 105 Great Russell Street, London WC1B 3RY
Tel 0171 636 1045 Fax 0171 636365. Mail Order.

SHELL WORK
Suppliers: Marine Arts Ltd, Long Rock Industrial Estate, Penzance, Cornwall TR20 8HX
Tel 01736 365169 Fax 01736 368545

Shell artist and garden designer: Emma Stable, Parget Cottage, Blakeney Road, Hindringham, Norfolk NR21 0BU
Tel 01328 830147

PAVING/SURFACES
Ammonites:Thomason Cudworth, The Old Vicarage, Cudworth, Ilminster, Somerset TA19 OPR
Tel 01460 57337 Fax 0146053737

Bonding of gravel with Bitumin emulsion: Colas Ltd, Wallage Lane, Rowfont, Crawley, West Sussex RH10 4NF
Tel 01342 711000

Breedon gravel: Breedon plc, Breedon on the Hill, Derby DE3 1AP
Tel 01332 862254

Crushed glass chippings: Derbyshire Aggregates (a wide range of colours) Arbor Low Works, Long Rake, Youlgrave Bakewell, Derbyshire DE45 1JS
Tel 01629 636500 Fax 01629 636425

Collyweston tile ends for end on use for paving: David Ellis, Collyweston Stone Slater, The Rosery, Ryhall, Stamford, Lincolnshire PE9 4HE
Tel 01780 763377

Glass beads: Dartington Crystal Ltd, Torrington, Devon EX38 7AN
Tel 01805 626262 Fax 01805 626263

Resin bonded gravel: Fibredec, Wallage Lane, Rowfont, Crawley, West Sussex RH10 4NF
Tel 01342 711000

Reproduction stone paving: Millstone Paving by Stonemarket, Old Gravel Quarry, Oxford Road, Ryton on Dunsmore, Warwickshire CV8 3EJ
Tel 01203 305530

Terracotta mosaics: Fired Earth Tiles plc, see Fired Earth plc under Paints and Woodstains

ADVICE ON TIMBER
Timber Research & Development Association (TRADA), Stocking Lane, Hughenden Valley, High Wycombe, Buckinghamshire HP14 4ND
Tel 01494 563091 Fax 01494 565487

DECKING, TRELLISWORK ETC
Lloyd Christie Garden Architecture, 1 New Kings Road, London SW6 4SB
Tel 0171 731 3484 Fax 0171 371 9952

SUPPLIERS OF COPPICED MATERIAL
Willow:
Steve Pick up, The Willow Bank, PO Box 17, Machynlleth, Powys SY20 8WR
Tel 01686 430510

Larry Jones c/o The Greenwood Trust, Station Road, Coalbrookdale, Telford, Shropshire TF8 7DR
Tel 01952 432769

Makers of furniture, fencing etc with coppiced wood: John Shone Pear Tree Cottage, Preston Hall, Preston, Oakham LE15 9NJ
Tel 01572 737438

WILLOW SCULPTURE, SEATS, ARBOURS AND TREEHOUSES
Clare Wilks, 76 Grafton Road, London NW5 3EJ
Tel 0171 284 1886

WILLOW WALLS AND BANKS
Green Wall, GSB Holdings plc, Surrey House, 39/41 High Street, Newmarket, Suffolk CB8 8NA
Tel 01638 668196 Fax 016638 668204

Land Conservation Associates, Model Farm, Crockham Hill, Edenbridge, Kent TN8 6SR
Tel 01732 866357 Fax 01732 866858

SOIL SUPPORT NETTING
(for stabilizing slopes until plants are established)
Tildenet GF4, Tildenet Ltd, Hartcliffe Way, Bristol BS3 5RJ
Tel 0117 966 9684 Fax 0117 923 1251

ROPES OF ALL SIZES
Footrope Knots, 501 Wherstead Road, Ipswitch, Suffolk IP2 8LL
Tel 01473 690090

SPECIALIST SUPPLIERS OF CARVED STONE ITEMS AND PAVING
English Limestone Products, 1a Wellington Lane, Stamford, Lincolnshire PE9 1QB
Tel 01780 764299

SCULPTURE GARDENS
Hannah Peschar Sculpture Garden, Ockley, Surrey
Tel 01306 627269

WOOD CARVER, FURNITURE MAKERS
David Williams, Studio One, Wyeside Workshops, Castle Street, Builth Wells, Powys LD2 3BY
Tel 01954 231533

FLINT SCULPTURES
Peter Gough, 13 Southover High Street, Lewes, East Sussex BN7 1HT
Tel 01273 472744

ARCHITECTS
Balston & Company see under Landscape Architects and Garden Designers

Robert Weighton, 10 Broad Street, Stamford, Lincolnshire
Tel 01780 481814 Fax 01780 481770

GARDEN BUILDINGS (Design and Build)
Buildings, sculpture, arbours or other items made from salvaged timber): Ben Wilson, 78a Colneyhatch Lane, London N1O 1EA
Tel 0181 444 3513

Mike Harvey, Goulters Mill Farm, The Gibb, Burton, Chippenham, Wiltshire
Tel 01249 782555

Richard Foxcroft, 2 Sunnyside, Woodend, Ardeley, Stevenage, Hertfordshire
Tel 01438 869444

PLAY EQUIPMENT
(including cable runways)
TP Activity Toys, available from stockists nationwide.

NATIONAL REGISTER OF MAKERS
Mosaics, furniture, sculpture, pebble work etc: The Crafts Council, 44a Pentonville Road, Islington, London N1 9BY
Tel 0171 278 7700 Fax 0171 837 6891

LIGHTING
Garden and Security Lighting, 70 New Wokingham Road, Crowthorne RG45 6JJ
Tel 01344 775 232

Outdoor Lighting, Unit 3, Kingston Business Centre, Fullers Way South, Chessington, Surrey KT9 1DQ
Tel 0181 974 2211 Fax 0181 974 2333

TOPIARY
Semi-mature pleached trees: Crown Topiary 234 North Road, Hertford SG14 2PW
Tel 01992 501055 Fax 01992 505142

Interesting frames and metal columns: Avant Garden, 77 Ledbury Road, London W11 2AG
Tel 0171 229 4408

Mature specimens: West Kington Nurseries, Pound Hill, West Kington, Chippenham, Wiltshire SN14 7JG
Tel 01249 782822

TREE AND SHRUB TIES
Special tape for tying in trees and shrubs when training: M.P. Richardson, 88 Valley Road, Rickmansworth, WD3 4BJ

FOUNTAINS AND WATER FEATURES
Water Techniques, Downside Mill, Cobham Park Road, Cobham, Surrey KT11 3PF
Tel 01932 866588 Fax 01932 860200

POTS
Woodhams, 60 Ledbury Road, London W11 2AJ
Tel 0181 964 9818 Fax 0181 964 9848

TERRACOTTA FINIALS
Finials made to order: Whichford Pottery, Nr Whychford, Shipston on Stour, Warwickshire CV6 5PG
Tel 01608 684416 Fax 01608 684833

RECONSTRUCTED STONE
Any stone sample colour matched: Grosvenor Stone, Golborne Bridge Farm, Handley, Chester CH3 9DR
Tel 01829 770632 Fax 01829 770642
Sculpture section, Judy Wiseman, 263 Nether Street, London N3 1PD

PATTERNED BRICKS
The York Handmade Brick Co Ltd, Forest Lane, Alne, North Yorkshire YO6 2LU
Tel 01347 838881

OLEOGRAPHY, REPRODUCTION PAINTINGS
Fine Masters, Five Hills, Bath, BA1 7JY
Tel 01225 859147

GEOTEXTILE MEMBRANE
(available from builders' merchants nationwide)
Manufactured by: Terram Ltd,
Tel 01495 757722 Fax 01495 762383